The Fontainebleau
Miami & Las Vegas

Ask A Local

Kevin &
Rebecca Plotner

4880 Lower Valley Road, Atglen, Pennsylvania 19310

Other Schiffer Books by Kevin & Becky Plotner
Ocean Drive Guidebook: Ask a Local. ISBN: 9780764328152.
$14.99
A Walking Tour of Lincoln Road, South Beach. ISBN:
9780764327216. $14.95

Other Schiffer Books on Related Subjects
Art Deco Architecture: Miami Beach Postcards. Paul
Clemence. ISBN: 0764323407. $9.95
Miami Memories: A Midcentury Journey. Mary L. Mar-
tin Tina Skinner & Nathaniel Wolfgang-Price. ISBN:
0764321765. $16.95
South Beach Architectural Photographs. Paul Clem-
ence with Foreword by Michael Hughes. ISBN:
0764320866. $24.95
South Beach: Faces and Facades. Iris Garnett Chase &
Gabriele Schuetz. ISBN: 0764325930. $24.95
South Beach Perspectives. Douglas Congdon-Martin.
ISBN: 9780764327964. $9.95

Copyright © 2008 by Kevin & Becky Plotner
Library of Congress Control Number: 2008931679

Designed by Mark David Bowyer
Type set in University Roman Bd BT / Zurich BT

ISBN: 978-0-7643-3016-2
Printed in China

Schiffer Books are available at special discounts for bulk
purchases for sales promotions or premiums. Special edi-
tions, including personalized covers, corporate imprints,
and excerpts can be created in large quantities for special
needs. For more information contact the publisher:

Published by Schiffer Publishing Ltd.
4880 Lower Valley Road
Atglen, PA 19310
Phone: (610) 593-1777; Fax: (610) 593-2002
E-mail: Info@schifferbooks.com

Please visit our web site catalog at
www.schifferbooks.com

We are always looking for
people to write books on new
and related subjects. If you have an idea for a book,
please contact us at the above address.

This book may be purchased from the publisher.
Include $5.00 for shipping.
Please try your bookstore first.
You may write for a free catalog.

In Europe, Schiffer books are distributed by:
Bushwood Books
6 Marksbury Ave.
Kew Gardens
Surrey TW9 4JF
England
Phone: 44 (0)208 392-8585
Fax: 44 (0)208 392-9876
E-mail: Info@bushwoodbooks.co.uk

Website: www.bushwoodbooks.co.uk
Free postage in the UK. Europe: air mail at cost.
Try your bookstore first.

Contents

Acknowledgments

The historical trail of Fontainebleau could not have been put into readable format without the help of countless people. Many, many people lived out their youth at the famous hotel but chose to remain nameless, and yet they told their story just to establish a historical trail. Thank you for your humility and your information.

Thank you Sarai Jiron, Paul Pebley, Linda Villafane, Stephen Muss, Liliam Hatfield, Richard Haas, Stuart Blumberg, Michael Aller, and the most loveable Lisa Cole. A special hats off goes to Katia Palatzo. Without your help and trustworthiness I would not be sane. Big thanks go to Kenneth Glenn, a big shot who shoots with dedication.

Most especially my everlasting summersaults to Gage and Cooper for all your assistance and encouragement. It's for you that my day exists. From your hair that is scared to the choices between A or B. It's to you that I dedicate this piece. Most high kudos goes to Captain X for whom words cannot describe the thanks. From notepads to a simple listening ear, you deserve the highest acknowledgment of all. To you, I curtsy while keeping eye contact.

Introduction

On December 20, 1954, the Fontainebleau changed the face of Miami Beach, transforming it to *the* hot spot and the grandest hotel of all time. The design of the hotel was unlike any other structure in the world. The décor inside was luxurious, extravagant, and breathtaking to the point where some visitors referred to it as "dizzying."

Celebrities and high profile guests flowed in and out of the entrance like the waves of the ocean. The lobby floor was polished every night to a high sheen while the rest of the hotel was primped regularly, ready for the perpetual debut. Employees worked diligently. Tips passed hands efficiently. Guests slept comfortably. Workers were treated with dignity. Profits were made.

This was the Fontainebleau. Volumes were spoken in the name, *Fontainebleau*. She screamed modern extravagance and good times. She had no competition. She stood alone on a level of rapport that didn't contend or struggle for the limelight; she defined limelight.

At the time, the rest of the beach was filled with low lying structures. The average building on the beach was a rectangle only a few stories tall. The land surrounding the Fontainebleau was filled with open space, sparse trees, grass desperately trying to take root in the sand, and sunshine. Enormous grand estates spattered the landscape north of Lincoln Road. Cookie cutter apartment houses filled the area south of Lincoln Road. Nationally known power players of the business world who came to Miami Beach to spend the winter owned the wealthy homes.

Chapter 1
The Firestone Estate

The first property to fill the current Fountainebleau grounds was The Firestone Estate. This enormous mansion caressed the shoreline at the area now bustling with Fontainebleau activity. The address, 4441 Collins Avenue, has always been a glamorous location positioned with prestige. This mansion was one of many in the area but was clearly the best of them all. People came out from miles and miles just to drive by the property and possibly get a peek inside the gate. **Millionaire's Row** was the term given to the strip of land in this area of Collins Avenue as the estates filled with millionaire businessmen lining the shore.

James Snowden, an oil tycoon from Oklahoma, built his home here at this site in 1907. At that time only a few smaller properties existed in the area surrounding his house. Snowden was the first millionaire to build a home on the ocean in Miami Beach. The three story mansion was an imposing home with fifteen bedrooms and six fireplaces, yes, fireplaces in Miami Beach. A high hedge that encompassed the home surrounded the estate. The entrance was made through towering gates that were always closed tight. The dominating entry opened up to the spacious estate's vast yard complete with a reflecting pool, ornamental landscaping, Italian Cypress trees, and decorative palms. The rectangular home was filled with ample sized windows fit to invite any possible ocean breeze into the home. The large home was seventeen oversized windows wide and six windows deep with space

to breathe and rooms to spare. Snowden had the sand built up prior to building the home so that it had a five-foot clearance from the top of the dunes in case of a storm surge.

This was clearly one of the first homes in the Miami Beach area. Henry Flagler came to the city of Miami to build the railroad in 1895. James Snowden massed his fortune with oil around the time Standard Oil, run by John D. Rockefeller, was taking over the market. Standard Oil became such a dominating force that the company was brought up on monopoly charges by the government but, in the mean time, their power forced other small companies like Snowden's to maintain a safe distance. Even so, James Snowden's wealth was abundant as was proven in this mansion.

The intersection of Collins Avenue and Indian Creek. The 37- story-tall Fontainebleau Tower stands on the right hand corner now.

In 1924, James Snowden leased out his home to **Harvey Samuel Firestone**. Shortly thereafter, Firestone purchased the home and the land soon became known as The Firestone Estate. The property was the best and grandest of the mansions in the area. Harvey, known to the locals as Harry, and his wife Elizabeth, were an upstanding addition to the beach. Big power families lived side by side, a horse's trot away from each other and the ocean. If you didn't have stables on your property, horses could be housed at one of several stables owned by pioneering developer Carl Fisher. He built them specifically for that reason.

Lindsey Hopkins, of the Coca-Cola family, had a home in the area, as did the Pancoasts. Thomas Pancoast married the daughter of Miami Beach pioneer developer John Collins, the man responsible for developing this region. Together with Collins, Pancoast put the area north of 22nd Street on the worldwide map. Common faces included J.C. Penny, Hertz, Florsheim, Maytag, Hoover, and the Vanderbilts. Over 600 millionaires called Miami Beach their winter hideaway. The 1930s were a quiet and peaceful time here on the beach. The area started to really pop in 1940 when 313 homes were added, as well as forty hotels. Word was getting out about the beach. Air travel was becoming more popular as airfares became more affordable. This opened up the ability for the average vacationer to travel to Miami, not just the super wealthy who could afford a two-day train ride from New York to Miami Beach.

As far back as you can go, Miami Beach was setting the pace as the destination to play. This morphed into a loose playground in a time of high fiber morals. In 1925 a minister was quoted in the *New York Times* saying, "If anyone wants to go to hell in a hurry there are greased banks aplenty in Miami."

Harvey Samuel Firestone (1868-1938) was most famous for his business dealings. Firestone Tire and Rubber Company was the first company to produce tires on the global market, which not only made his family wealthy, but also launched the economy of America into a new level of trade. Firestone's rubber came from trees worldwide, specifically from his own rubber plantation in Liberia where they farmed one million acres of timber.

The Firestone Estate was purchased from Snowden four years after this 1920 photo.

Firestone was part of a rat pack of his own in his day as he, **Thomas Edison**, and **Henry Ford** were the trio of friends known to work together and vacation together. Collectively they kept company with two neighbors, Fisher and Sieberling, who lived at the foot of Lincoln Road with their palatial homes located where the Ritz and Decoplage now reside. Carl Fisher made his millions as the man responsible for putting the headlight to market as well as building the famous Brickyard racetrack in Indianapolis. F.A. Sieberling made his millions as President of Goodyear Tire and Rubber Company. Add Fisher's vacationing friend Charles F. Kettering, inventor of the self-starter that replaced the hand crank to start the early automobiles, and you've got yourself a collection of men who literally put the automobile on the map. Million dollar world-changing deals were made between Firestone, Ford, and Edison with simple words, no contracts, and often not even a handshake.

When you picture these car tycoons hanging out at the beach it makes you wonder what they would think of the vast number of Lamborghinis, Bentleys, and Ferraris we have dominating Miami Beach today.

The Snowden mansion was bought by Firestone in 1924 after the short lease. He called the home **Herbal Villa,** as it was a medicinal place of relaxation by the sea for the hardworking man.

Firestone paid $250,000 for the home in 1924. That year the average yearly income was $1,124 and the average median home price was $7,720. A pound of steak cost 41 cents and a stamp would set you back 2 cents. This was the first year in history that every car at the National Automobile Show had a gasoline engine; steam power was taking the back shelf. The residential population on Miami Beach was 6,419 with the heaviest numbers down on South Beach. The area here at 4400 Collins was extremely rural as little existed out here. In 1928 the *Miami Daily News* reported the average lot in the Millionaire's Row area was running $225,000. (Kleinberg, 1987)

Harvey Firestone died here in the estate at the age of 69 from coronary thrombosis, a heart attack, while sleeping.

After Harvey's death, the Firestones didn't come to the house as much and then the Second World War separated the connection further. The vacation home no longer held its allure for the Firestone family. The once beautiful property, no longer a hotspot for Harvey Firestone's descendants, slowly fell into disuse.

Comparative prices were not as easy to find at that time as they are now. A neighboring property sold circa 1940 for $205,000 with 235 feet of oceanfront. The Firestone's were not financially strapped but they wanted to sell nonetheless.

The heirs to the Firestone Estate desired a large apartment complex or hotel but were stopped by **zoning restrictions**. The family took the City of Miami Beach to court in 1950 but the city prevailed. To ease the Firestone heirs' dilemma, the city's response was an offer to buy their property. The offer was $1 million, but the family wanted no less than $1.4 million. A counter offer came from the city with the same value but for a smaller section of the property. This was turned down by the heirs. (Stofik 2005, 46)

Unknown to the Firestones, the area in front of the house, on the beach, was used as an impromptu modeling studio while they waited for a purchase agreement. Bunny Yeager, a model in the early 1950s, began taking her own photographs, even of herself modeling. "Most of those early photos were shot on a little beach behind the old Firestone estate that later became the Fontainebleau." (Biondi 2007, 90) Yeager began taking photos of models with exotic bikinis. The bikinis were an eye-opening experience for the viewing public. At the time, proper photo swimsuits were made by Jantzen and provided full coverage, low on the leg and high on the chest. Such swimsuits included fancy skirts to provide more discreet coverage.

Bunny Yeager is not only responsible for her famous modeling, photography, and self-made bathing suits. She took photos of Betty Page in her famously captivating Santa hat. Bunny made the hat by sewing fake white fur to a red Santa hat. She posed Betty Page holding a large red ball, wearing the Santa hat … and nothing else. Bunny sent the photos to Hugh Hefner, a young new magazine publisher at the time. Young Hefner was twenty-seven years old that year in 1953 and had just put out his first issue of the controversial magazine *Playboy*. He had the fortitude to, "gamble $500 on his first cover girl – an unknown Hollywood wannabe named Marilyn Monroe." (Buck Wolf, ABCNews.com) Hefner fell in love with Bunny Yeager's shots, so Bunny invited Hugh to Miami Beach and showed him the town. Bunny became a well-known photographer shooting photos for *Playboy Magazine.*

Chapter 2
Ben Novack

In 1952 **Ben Novack bought the property for $2.3 million**. The land was 950 feet long at the beach and 350 feet deep from the ocean to Indian Creek. The wait proved successful for the Firestone heirs but, "The next day, Ben was offered $3,500,000 for (the Firestone Estate) and turned it down." (Bishop 1961)

As a price comparison, in 1956 a property in the 68th Street and Collins area was leased by Alfred Kaskel. Kaskel was a developer of many large apartment buildings in Queens and a handful of small hotels in Manhattan. Kaskel leased the property for $200,000 a year on a 99-year-lease. (Schneider 1956) The 99-year-lease was a popular method of leaving property to your heirs with a renter covering the cost of the taxes while you sat on the asset.

The elaborate and enormous Firestone Estate was made into the **offices and headquarters** for Ben Novack during construction of the Fontainebleau. Ben took the formal dining room that overlooked the ocean for his own personal office space and gave the billiards room to Duke Stewart, the hotel manager. The billiards room was formerly a popular place for President Warren G. Harding to spend the evening while he visited his friends the Firestones. (Flynn 1954) When the hotel was near full completion, the Novack family moved into their blocked off suites inside the hotel, the Firestone Estate was leveled, and the extravagant Fontainebleau gardens were planted.

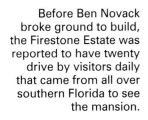

Before Ben Novack broke ground to build, the Firestone Estate was reported to have twenty drive by visitors daily that came from all over southern Florida to see the mansion.

Before the developer broke ground on the Fontainebleau, America had suffered many long years through the Depression and then through World War II. People were ready to let their hair down and kick up their heels. Latin music was a sound seldom heard in America but was a growing commodity here in Miami Beach. The beat made your hips gyrate as it begged you to get up off your chair.

Prior to the Fontainebleau's oversized famous curve, hotels were smaller in scale and simple. Boxes, rectangles, and simple lines made up the exterior of apartment buildings and hotels that stood a few stories tall. A handful of exceptions graced the skyline but they were far from the 4000 block of Collins Avenue. The Fontainebleau stood out not only for its drastic difference in architecture but because it was huge in the sea of low lying rooftops.

When the original plan for the hotel was published, the Fontainebleau was to be a **550 room hotel**. This was just for the one building, the original curved structure that made up the hotel. At the time, this was an enormous size for Miami Beach. Most hotels were small, hovering around the four-story level. No other grand hotel existed on Miami Beach.

This is a difficult visual when today the original curved building is massively dwarfed by the towering 37-story Fontainebleau Suites Tower. This is the same original curved building that massively dwarfed everything else around it at the time it was built.

Ben Novack ordered the décor to be **French Provincial**, a style established in the 17th and 18th centuries. French Provincial décor was not just functional; it was elegant and stylish as it displayed the riches of life. A mirror wasn't just a mirror, it was a mirror framed with a sweeping gilded impression of vines and waves that crashed and danced with flowing grace. Each piece, whether it was a building or a table, was elaborately made, containing the presence of history and romance.

Novack planned for a 32,000 square foot ballroom with over 5,000 person occupancy. He wanted the hotel to become a casino but the heavy hand of legal regulations altered the plans. For a short time in 1935 slot machines were legalized in the Miami Beach area, but the legalized gambling didn't last long. The ruling was rescinded in November of 1936. Ben Novack was hoping the tide would turn in his favor and legalized gambling would grant him the hotel he desired. He had

hopes for his new venture, but there is no true evidence that he imagined his grand hotel would house world-changing events like the Republican National Convention, as well as the Democratic National Convention.

Ben Novack came from a family familiar with hotels. In the Catskills region of New York, Ben's father owned Laurel-in-the-Pines, better known as The Laurels, a famous resort on Sacket Lake. He grew up knowing the business and combined two fields into one when he became a developer. Still, today, it's not common practice to be a builder and an hotelier; usually the two are separate entities. This fact proved a total asset to Novack on many levels. It allowed knowledge to intertwine with knowledge.

Ben Novack was a hard dealing businessman who carried a big bark and a firm opinion which took skill to waver. He hung around with the big boys like Frank Sinatra and Howard Hughes on a regular basis. Novack was known to be hard of hearing and often caused some high volume conversations. He loved his wife with a passion and fervor. One time for her birthday he changed all the faucets and fittings in their Fontainebleau apartment to gold as a surprise.

In 1940 Novack started his Miami Beach career with $1,800 in his pocket. His first building adventure was a lease on the Monroe Towers for $10,000, which he didn't have so he pulled two partners along with him. He bought the place shortly thereafter for $168,000. This was just prior to when the military moved into town and occupied the majority of the Miami Beach hotels as barracks. Novack sold the place to the Army with an admirable profit and turned to his next lease with the Cornell Hotel. He sold the lease, making a handsome profit, and then moved on to purchasing the Atlantis for $500,000. In 1947 he sold the Atlantis for $1.5 million. Ben then went into partnership with two other men and bought the Sans Souci for $3 million. He sold the Sans Souci for $4.65 million "and kept the title to the land under it." (Bishop 1961)

From the Sans Souci, Ben Novack promptly moved on to buying the Firestone Estate for $2.3 million. He built the hotel on the land for $13.5 million and then turned around and added another $4 million in upgrades shortly thereafter. Architect Morris Lapidus was paid $65,000.

Local **hotelier Stuart Blumberg** said, "Novack was an entrepreneur. Ben was way before his time. He envisioned things that none of us had even thought about." This was evident in the boldest way when Novack made it possible to have retail shops and a nightclub in the hotel. That was illegal until Novack came around. He changed the law to meet the needs of his hotel. He tried to do the same with the gaming industry but never reached success on the concept of gambling.

Stuart Blumberg explained the fact that, historically, hoteliers are pressure cookers. Ben Novack was a perfect example of the kettle blowing his top at frequent intervals. The job in itself involves high stress, piggy backing a high blood pressure, high alcoholism, and high divorce rate.

A true taste of Ben Novack is best described with one informative story. One local family lived in the hotel year round as a way to clear an outstanding debt. As partial reimbursement of that debt, a residence was established for the family. As a result, Michael Aller grew up in the Fontainebleau hotel, where he lived with his family, and remembered one day just like any other. He was sitting in the cafe eating his marble cake when he heard gunshots – in the hotel.

Young Aller shot up from his table with his teenager's agility and ran toward the sound of the shots. Everyone was in an uproar with the commotion. Michael Aller said, "Hotel security grabbed me and made a big fuss about getting me out of there – my father would kill them if they let me through." As the story goes, Ben Novack found out his wife was cheating on him with the orchestra director, Papi Compo. Bernice Novack was a *beautiful* woman and a former model in New York. Novack took his gun to where the orchestra was playing, pointed his gun directly at the leader and the next thing everyone knew, two shots were fired into the ceiling.

Novack's rage saw no borders when he fired his gun inside the fully occupied hotel. This incident is an excellent definitive description to Novack's character.

When you ask people who personally knew Ben Novack about his character, you'll get an earful. Local Michael Aller thought deep and hard to find praise and said, "Ben Novack built the most beautiful and grand hotel of the time."

Still Novack was a powerful businessman. He pushed and orchestrated events that filled the halls with visitors. He wasn't just a builder, he was a true hotelier. The Fontainebleau was an enormous success. It was known throughout the world as the most glorious hotel on the market. At that time, there was no competition in this field of resort extravagance. Ben Novack had such a hit on his hands that he **never even put up a sign** in front of the hotel heralding the name Fontainebleau. "Novack's idea has always been to make something so stupendous that it would identify itself." (Redford, 1970 p 241)

In the book *Learning from Las Vegas*, architect Robert Venturi refers to this level of market domination as Signs and Systems where the building itself *is* the sign. When the building becomes the sign, total recognition is itself extreme market placement.

The expense to buy the land and build the Fontainebleau was hefty. In 1961 a strait shooting reporter and hotel enthusiast named Bishop wrote, "Novack must take in $12,000,000 a year to make the place pay. He can do this with 60 per cent room occupancy, and the Fontainebleau has averaged 78 per cent. So he's solvent. In fact, out of $20,000,000 in costs, Mr. Novack owes the bank only $7,500,000. He owns 72 per cent of his hotel and has two mystery partners."

Working from these numbers, Ben Novack came to Miami Beach in 1940 with $1,800 and had an asset fortune of $20 million 15 years later in 1955.

This capitalization of funds was not due to his graceful, elegant character. Novack pulled the French proper name of Fontainebleau to Miami Beach but he never wavered on the pronunciation of his own hotel. Novack forced out the words saying, "Fountain Blue."

After his ventures at the Fontainebleau proved successful for Ben, he tried to reinvent himself. He was making a handsome profit of $2 million a year when the hotel was going strong. Still, he wanted to break into the **lucrative venture of gambling**. As gaming was illegal in Miami Beach, this meant one thing; he needed to seek another location. He tried to sell his concept for a Fontainebleau resort and casino in the area of Cat Cay, Bahamas. The Bahamian government did their homework and found an inauspicious personality in Ben Novack. They "refused to grant him a license, citing, 'unfavorable police information on his character'." (Cohen 2002) He continued his plan by attempting to open his venture in Tel Aviv creating a Fontainebleau Israel, again, right on the water. This didn't pan out either.

All the while, Ben Novack was planning another Miami venture with a couple of local developers. They were planning a new golf resort on the property west of the airport that would float on the tailwinds of the Fontainebleau. The development of this 440-acre track of land was an enormous undertaking, both financially and strategically.

This golf resort would be more of a town in it's own quadrant, complete with road systems, apartment buildings, condominium complexes, parks, and schools.

Things began to unravel for Novack as a hearty group of probing reporters were doing everything they knew to expose his suspected connection to the mob. Published reports were made again and again. Ben Novack held firm on his innocence. Eventually he won his lawsuit against *The Miami Herald* where the paper ran a report on the front page. The two paragraphs didn't officially say, "We were wrong," or, "We apologize." Instead, the paper wrote, in a nutshell, that it was *the opinion of the paper* that no underworld business dealings owned or ran the hotel. The description of the lawsuit being put to bed by that very same article was longer than the "retraction" that defamed Novack and his character. As reports normally go, the damage to Novack at that time was severe. Added to his personality traits, high volume encounters, and gruff business mannerisms, he was seeing more and more convention cancellations and vacancies than he could control.

With all his attempted business ventures, Novack's financial situation was stretched thin. Total failure for Novack's Fontainebleau was seen when he was a full $5 million behind in his mortgage payments. (Stofik 2005, 46) This snowballed to complete financial failure with the solemn result of a court ordered removal from control at the Fontainebleau. Bankruptcy tumbled to Novack's doorstep.

As far as business went, Ben Novack accomplished a lot throughout his lifetime. *The New York Times* wrote his obituary on April 7, 1985, saying, "Mr. Novack had been at the center of a mental competency fight over his ability to administer his estate, estimated at $1 million." The story had more to it when they added, "A week ago, Mr. Novack's son, Ben Novack Jr., asked a Miami judge to find his father mentally incompetent to handle his finances and to appoint a legal guardian. But Juana M. Rodriguez, who said she lived with Mr. Novack for five years, objected to the move by his son, saying he had improperly obtained a power of attorney from his father. (She) said the younger Mr. Novack had kept his father over-sedated and denied him access to his friends." Miss Rodriguez was thirty years old at the time of Novack Sr.'s death and was noted as the former Miss Uruguay.

Chapter 3
Morris Lapidus

Fontainebleau architect Morris Lapidus was born in Odessa, Russia, in 1903 and came to America with his parents when he was a toddler. He grew up in the Lower East Side of New York before it became a ghetto. His family worked hard and stressed the importance of values and morals. His father, Leon Lapidus, worked as a coppersmith, where he made carbide headlight housings. This was ironic as the land here on Miami Beach in 1910 was being developed by Carl Fisher, the man that put the headlight to market. Lapidus' father was eventually promoted to partner. Lapidus grew up with many dreams but not a lot of money. He knew how to work hard and more importantly he knew how to talk to people.

In school he desired to act on stage and pursued his passion through set design. Lapidus sought his degree at Columbia University School of Architecture and then began working in a firm where his first job was designing the bathrooms for the Atlantic City Convention Hall. "For two weeks I did nothing but draw toilets." (Lapidus 1996, 65) This act of menial repetition and mundane purpose propagated enormous frustration for Lapidus; he decided to seek another position. As he was handing in his resignation, he was handed a project to calm his irritation and occupy his time. This project was to look over the plans of a current job and see if everything fit. As a result of this, he designed a plaster ornament that was used as the emblem to William K. Vanderbilt's garage in Long Island. From there his specific job was to design retail shops.

He worked for the firm credited with designing Grand Central Station, Ross-Frankel. From 1929-1943, **Lapidus designed 450 retail stores**. He focused on his designs from one angle; design a project that the people wanted. He studied the way people shopped and built the store around the customer's habits. He saw that they were attracted to light and designed plans to meet that desire, and called it the moth complex. He saw they meandered through a store as they shopped, so he made the design with a sweeping, curving flow. He used col-ors to attract attention and built the structure in a user-friendly manner.

Lapidus wanted to present the merchandise to the shopper so he made the whole storefront a glass showcase filled with light to display the eye-catching items on sale. It was a free point of product advertising and he used it to the fullest potential. Before Lapidus, storefronts were brick walls with doors. He purposefully designed and labeled certain aspects intentional nonsense, things purposefully designed to pull people in and guide them through a store. He did this to push people past lingering spots to an area of desire. He designed around customers' subconscious, curiosity, and pleasure.

During his honeymoon to the Caribbean, Lapidus and his new wife, Beatrice Perlman, encountered a layover in Miami. They fell in love with the area and decided to return. Lapidus remembered this first visit to Miami with fondness as it was during the time of Prohibition. His new wife Bea liked rum and snuck a few bottles along tucked in her girdle. Everything was good and fine until the doorman dressed to perfection helped Bea out of the taxi. At that exact moment one of her hidden bottles, "escaped and plopped to the pavement. The sweet smell of rum filled the warm, balmy air. While I paid the fare, she ran toward the hotel entrance, only to have two more bottles crash to the sidewalk. This was our grand entry to Miami Beach." (Lapidus 1996, 85) In 1947, working in both New York and Miami, he moved to Miami but continued his New York to Miami commute.

As a young boy, Morris Lapidus was hit by a car and suffered tragically while his body recovered in the hospital. He was very young and very frightened. He learned two main things from the incident. One he learned the hard way as a lawyer came to visit the family in the hospital and had Morris' father sign papers for protection. As it turned out that lawyer was legal representation for the responsible party that hit young Morris and his father signed away any ability to sue. The second lesson was that of color and how it made him feel. "Years later I realized that my love of color came from the beautiful field of colorful wildflowers that had been absorbed in my subconscious and that the green hospital room has kept me from ever using green." (Lapidus 1996, 44)

Over the course of his lifetime Lapidus put his fingers and talent on **1,200 different projects** including open-air malls, resort hotels, condominiums, hospitals, synagogues, and performing arts centers.

In his later years and long after his death, Lapidus was fondly remembered by those who knew him. Laura Lauer, a longtime Miami Beach resident, lived in the same building as Morris Lapidus for many years and described him as "a refined socially acceptable and palatable person." The building where he lived, Terrace Towers, is located at 3 Island Avenue, directly on Biscayne Bay, and welcomes breathtaking sunsets as well as views of the bay. Lauer described Lapidus as a gentleman of the old school. "Very rarely did I see him without a blue blazer. Only once did I see him in short sleeves. He was impeccable. A starched gentleman."

Lapidus lived in his duplex apartment with his wife of sixty-three happy years. He was described as a one-woman man who treated ladies with dignity and grace. The building was designed by Lapidus himself, so he chose the plan to his own personal apartment. By combining two, two-bedroom apartments, he created a true home connecting two levels with a circular staircase. "He was a real bon vivant," Laura Lauer described. "He was very quiet, soft spoken, and gentlemanly. He had his assistant drive him when he was no longer able in his years. Still, he was as sharp as ever until the end." Morris Lapidus was fondly remembered as a gentleman who always had a kind smile and a soft hello for passersby. Lapidus passed away at the age of ninety-eight on January 18, 2001, nine years after his wife Beatrice.

Morris Lapidus was most popular for his architecture but put an even bigger stamp on the world through **his son, Alan Lapidus,** who himself became an architect. Alan has designed many successful projects for prominent figures of today like Donald Trump, Aristotle Onassis, the CIA, and Disney. He has most recently written a book entitled *Everything By Design* that is praised as an entertaining, enjoyable, and easy read.

As Morris Lapidus started his building designing career, he had no idea he was entering stormy waters. Laughter and smiles didn't always fill the rooms and corridors of the Fontainebleau, especially behind closed doors in the office. On the contrary, during the designing and building of the hotel, the attitude was much different. Not only was there a difference, but also the squabble set many a conversation a twirl for many moons thereafter. Ben Novack hired the up and coming Russian architect, Morris Lapidus, to put the face and makeup on the hotel. Young on the hotel scene, Lapidus was an economical find for Novack. Morris Lapidus had his hand in the design of several buildings already including the Sans Souci in 1947, the Nautilus in 1950, the Algiers in 1951, the Biltmore Terrace in 1951, and the DiLido, also in 1951. The design of the Fontainebleau was Morris Lapidus' first lead architect position where he ran the show.

The desire for Ben Novack was simple, he wanted a hotel aura to attract the high class attitude of the shoppers that frequented Lincoln Road. Lincoln Road at the time was a traditional street. The City of Miami Beach hired Morris Lapidus to transform the street into a pedestrian thoroughfare in 1960 with a budget of $600,000. Lapidus was commonly known as the man who saw what people wanted, then designed the project to fill the need.

Sadly, Novack and Lapidus didn't have a smooth and peaceful working relationship; they often bucked in design. The two men had many conversations appropriate for any theater screen. The curve of the building, a groundbreaking design of the time, was often the topic.

Lapidus designed new forms, new shapes, and new ideas. He became well known for his inconsistency with tradition and rules. Instead, his designs contained interjected shapes, holes, patterns, and waves, that broke up the flowing wall. He used columns that didn't perform a function but were solely intended as decoration. They were thin and decorative with gold fluted feathers bursting from the top as the pole met the ceiling. Lapidus loved curves and angles. He said, "I always hated long corridors where the line of sight was so exhausting. So I curved the corridor, making an apparently never-ending walkway." (Desilets 2004, 8) Later in his years he was on a walking tour with Fontainebleau Director of Public Relations, Lisa Cole, when he told her he made the curve with the visual of only a handful of rooms at a time. This enabled the guests to feel like their room and their space was personal and dedicated to them instead of the feeling that they were in a massive hotel.

Typical architecture of the time was geometrical in shape. Simple boxes formed buildings. Linear corners met squares and rectangles for a completed, clean look. Morris Lapidus liked the flow of curves, holes, and zigzag shapes. He was thinking outside the box in his design flare. He shook up the world of architecture, broke all the traditional rules of design, and set the stage for a new era.

The dominating size of the chateau dwarfed other surrounding hotels. Elaborate décor accompanied spacious common areas.
Courtesy of Fontainebleau.

Before the Fontainebleau, architectural forms were mostly rectangular in shape.
Courtesy of Fontainebleau.

The beachfront was swamped with Fontainebleau cabanas in 1954.
Courtesy of Fontainebleau.

Chapter 4
The Working Relationship

The association between Morris Lapidus and Ben Novack was one that started off from day one as a relationship that took work. When Morris Lapidus was asked to design a plan for the 1949 Sans Souci hotel by a group of partners, he thought it would be smooth sailing with the group. Lapidus had a friendly working relationship with Charlie Spector, an architect and then vice-president to A.S. Beck Shoe Store chain. Lapidus was connected to Charlie when designing shoe stores in New York. Charlie introduced Lapidus to his friend in Miami Beach, Ben Novack. At the time Ben was building a hotel at the beach and was not fully happy with the architectural plans received for the building so he decided to inquire about ideas from Charlie. Charlie matched up Novack's visions with Lapidus' alternative design flare. Novack asked Charlie for input and Charlie, in turn, asked Lapidus for input. This was the introduction forming the connection of Ben Novack and Morris Lapidus. Charlie told Novack, "(Morris Lapidus) had a dramatic flair for creating exciting and attention-compelling structures and interiors." (Lapidus 1979, 125)

Lapidus wrote, "I have always abhorred a straight line and more so the rectangle." When asked of his hotel design experience, "I told Ben that I had stayed at hotels but that actually I had never designed a hotel. I didn't bother to mention that once I had desinged [sic] a hotel years ago in which I had forgotten to put bathrooms in each guest room. Since that hotel had never been built, I could not claim that I had, in fact, designed a hotel." At their meeting, Morris Lapidus grabbed some wrapping paper that was handy, and began adding to the hotel's design.

Straight lines were not part of Morris Lapidus' design plan. This broke the rules of architecture while it established an irresistible flow. *Courtesy of Fontainebleau.*

He added a "circular drive to dramatize the entrance," and altered the lobby to, "be shaped with various sweeping curves and that the space be broken up by terraces with a number of levels." Lapidus understood that sweeping curves added excitement and flare, light attracted people, and multiple levels divided by a few stairs created diversity. It produced architectural eye candy, intrigue, and amusement for the human eye. It brought out the internal child in grown adults, fulfilling their subliminal desires to crawl under a blanket-made fort and wander through a maze.

As Lapidus sketched out plans on the wrapping paper, he explained how he was creating relaxed luxury with flowing curves and sweeping mediums. This allowed people to internally explode with giddy excitement and break away from their everyday rut. It created a true vacation aura.

Lapidus was used to designing store fronts where he sold merchandise. With that same angle he sold fun and enthusiasm.

"Novack was very impressed. He asked me what I would charge as my fee for acting as the interior designer of the hotel, and also as a consultant with his architect on the design of the entire building. I suggested a fee of $15,000. I knew that the fee was too low. Novak's comment was that the fee was entirely too high and he was sorry to have taken up my time." (p. 126)

Shortly thereafter, Harry Mufson called Morris Lapidus. Harry was Ben Novack's business partner on the Sans Souci project. Harry had no issue with Lapidus' reasonable fee and Morris Lapidus was on his path to designing his first hotel, the Sans Souci. The project took place in Miami Beach with business partners Ben Novack, Harry Mufson, and an apparel manufacturer, also named Harry.

One problem ensued. The architect already established on the Sans Souci was not too polite when he saw Morris Lapidus' sketches for the hotel. This architect was a solid designer, one who had designed a vast majority of the hotels already on Miami Beach. He knew his architecture and he knew how to design his hotels. "The architect startled us all by saying that everything that I had designed was impractical and in short, could not be built. He insisted that there were to be no changes in the plans." (p. 126) The hotel's architect, a formidable man, made it plain he didn't take too favorably to Lapidus' designs. This raised enormous doubts in the Harry, Harry, and Ben partnership. After hearing their architect's complaints, Morris Lapidus, in the eyes of the partners, was instantly reduced to a wide-eyed visionary drawing out dreams and clouds, instead of a schooled and skilled architect.

Harry, Harry, and Ben didn't know architecture. There seemed to be only one solution, contact a knowledgable architect. Charlie Spector was called from New York to see if the plans were plausible and structurally sound.

After thorough study, Charlie, a famous architect in his own right, asked the disgruntled architect if he possessed an architectural license.

"Yes."

Charlie responded, "Then I suggest, Sir, that you surrender your license. I have never heard such nonsense before from a man who professes to be a practicing architect." (p. 127)

Morris Lapidus was then asked to design the whole project. He was thrilled with the job, but learned later it was not all to be smooth sailing. Arguing was often an aspect of the planning process as the three cooks in the kitchen often took different opinions on their ideas. Lapidus was caught in the middle but accomplished the work on a consensus vote.

Lapidus wrote about the squabble regarding the Sans Souci that set the table for the coming feast:

There was a feeling of fellowship and mutual agreement until Big Harry suggested that the nightclub be designed as a big, brassy adjunct for the hotel. "Let's really pull out all the stops."

"I don't agree. I want a small, intimate club – nothing big and brassy," said Ben.

"I think you're wrong, Ben. Let's make our hotel a jumping place," Big Harry replied.

"And I say, keep it small and intimate." Ben again.

"I agree with Harry; make it big and brassy," Little Harry joined the argument.

"Look, you two, I'm the hotel man. You stick to the tire business, and you stick to making dresses. I've decided it's going to be small and intimate and that's that!"

"Wait a minute, Ben, I'm a partner. Don't give me any of that crap about the tire business. I've been around more hotels as a guest than you have, and I say make it big."

"Who cares what you say? I'm gonna run this hotel and what I say goes! Make it small and intimate, Morris. Don't listen to these two jokers."

"Waddya mean, jokers." (Little Harry speaking.) "We're equal partners and we've got as much to say as you have, Mr. Big-Shot Hotel Operator."

"Nuts to you, I'm calling the shots. Stick to your dresses."

"Screw you, Ben. We're partners and we've decided by vote. It's two against one, so make it big, Morris."

Then the fur began to fly, and the air became blue with more four-letter words than I knew existed. Charlie tried to make peace, but to no avail. Ben grabbed his wife and told her, "We're getting the hell out of here. I'm through. The deal is off. Let's go!" (p. 128-129)

As far as arguing went, this was one of many disagreements. The result proved one thing, Ben Novack was a strong businessman with stronger opinions, and solid arguing skills.

It wasn't just Lapidus, or his business partners, that Novack argued with, it was everyone. The *Miami Herald* did a piece on the beach erosion problem in the late '60s and put two quotes in large, bold text. One was from Mayor Jay Dermer, the father to our most recent Miami Beach three-term mayor, Mayor David Dermer. Mayor Jay told the paper, "Miami Beach is the nation's most graphic example of hotel owners stealing the beaches."

Ben Novack's response was, "You bring me anybody in Miami Beach who says we're short of beach. Show me just one – outside of the jerk mayor." (Donated clipping)

From the Sans Souci, Ben Novack jumped to build the Fontainebleau on a vast span of property consisting of twenty-two acres.

At that time, Morris Lapidus was in New York **reading a newspaper** and discovered the information about Ben's new project in Miami. Shockingly to Morris, he also read that he himself was the architect for this new luxury hotel going up on the shore of Miami Beach. This was news to Lapidus, as he had not heard of the project until that point. As most individuals would have done, Morris Lapidus made a phone call to Ben Novack and found Novack was open to having Lapidus on the job but he hadn't chosen his main architect to run the project. In a knee jerk response from a questioning reporter Ben mentioned Morris Lapidus as his architect without much thought. He was open to working with Morris but hadn't chosen an architect to design the whole structure.

Morris Lapidus saw a window of opportunity and stated that he could be the lead architect. He sold himself and gave Ben Novack little opportunity to choose another candidate.

In his first sketch to Novack proposing the now famous curve of the building the hotel was referred to as "Estates" after the Firestone Estate property on which it sat.

When Lapidus met with Novack to show him his first ideas, Morris Lapidus had twenty-seven drawings prepared, each with a curve. When Novack saw the drawings he tore them up saying, "I want a hotel."

The main plug that got Morris Lapidus the job was, as most things go, settled in on money. Traditional fees for architectural work at the time were commissions of 4% of the structure's cost. At a projected building cost of $12 million, the architectural fee should have been $480,000. In their agreement, Morris Lapidus allowed his fee to be cut to $80,000. This covered Morris' payment for all architectural drawings and sketches, engineering, and interior design. To get the job, Lapidus waved the standard fee of 4% and brought it down to roughly 0.65%. At the time he offered himself for such a low fee he considered and weighed the potential prospects of bankruptcy. He decided to gamble with his commission, using the opportunity to show the world his architectural skills.

Chapter 5
The Graceful Flowing Curve

The originating concept of the Fontainebleau curve has come to be regarded as having ignited one of the largest arguments of Miami Beach history. The notion of who designed the famous curve has been disputed since before day one of hotel construction.

Morris Lapidus wrote two autobiographies, *An Architecture of Joy,* and *Too Much is Never Enough.* Both books are well written, clear, and entertaining. More importantly, both tell different details that line up the same overlapping stories to perfection. Not one recalled event differed on any note. Lapidus' memory was sharp and his people skills were sharper. He described how he presented twenty-six architectural drawings to Ben Novak on potential styles for the Fontainebleau. Each of the twenty-six drawings had some version of a sweeping curve in various formats. Lapidus reported that after twenty-six drawings, Ben Novack had an epiphany. "Why not have a curved building? No one has ever designed a curved building."

One of Lapidus' employees commented on Morris' love for a curve as it made the walkway appear as if it never ended. It added an invigorating concept instead of an exhausting feel.

"I had practically pushed curved buildings down his gullet, and now it had become his inspiration. Did I tell him that I had been trying to get him to accept a curved building all along? What for? I had gotten what I wanted." (Lapidus 1979, 138)

When you talk to the locals, even today, you'll find a bit of a riff still floating through the air. The Novack family members are easily forthright to inform that Ben Novack designed the curve of the Fontainebleau. They are bluntly candid in fact. Novack's then wife, Bernice, and her son, Benny Jr., tell the same tale. As she describes it, Ben was on the toilet for an excessively long span of time one morning. After literally an hour and a half of what I like to call *private contemplation on the can* at the Sans Souci one morning, he emerged with three pages of building sketches. I would lie if I said I didn't type this with a smile on my face because

the beautiful and glamorous Bernice, with the look of a beauty queen, commented on his exit from the toilet by saying, "He liked things that are round, like the feeling of embracing arms."

Benny Jr., Bernice, and Ben Novack's son were asked about the curve by famous professors, historians, and authors Stuart Blumberg and Howard Kleinberg. The response from Benny was close-lipped, as he desired to write his own book about his dad. He claimed the curve came from Ben and only Ben; any other notion was absurd. He claims he himself has the original plans from the toilet incident in a secure and hidden away safe. When the professors asked if they could see these plans, Benny Jr. brushed them off. He didn't want to open the safe.

Morris Lapidus printed it differently in his book *An Architecture of Joy*, "At each step of the way, my client insisted that he would do the designing and I, to use his oft-repeated phrase, 'was to push the pencil'. I was determined that I was not going to become a pencil pusher for my client: I would just let him think that everything I did was really an idea of his." (Lapidus 1979, 136)

It was right around this time that the choppy flow of planning and preparing to break ground lurched to a standstill. The abrupt halt in progress was caused by one event: a lawsuit. "The two Harrys, who seemed so pleased to see their one-time partner go into a new venture, sued him. The suit claimed that, since he had used partnership funds to purchase the Firestone Estate he was bound to take the two Harrys with him as his partners." (Lapidus 1979, 139) It was later reported that Harry Mufson was the instigator of the lawsuit.

All progress on the Fontainebleau that could be done without breaking ground went forward. Everything else stopped. Lapidus continued to create plans and make drawings. He set up his office in Miami Beach as a satellite office to his New York location and continued to staff both locations. Many plane flights were made back and forth from Miami to New York and the drawings were all perfected, ready for the build. A whole year of work with no physical evidence of a building added a bit of dramatic tension to the project.

While the lawsuit was brewing, unbeknownst to Ben Novack, Harry Mufson had been working out a deal to purchase the land directly north of Fontainebleau. If he couldn't be part of the Fontainebleau project, he was going to build a hotel right next to the Fontainebleau and it would outshine anything Novack could throw together.

Building restrictions remained in place on both properties while the lawsuit was active. Once settled, the Fontainebleau could break ground. This also meant Mufson's Eden Roc hotel could break ground. It was reported that this was the reason Harry Mufson dropped the lawsuit.

The **Fontainebleau broke ground** and made record breaking progress on the build. Up until this time, Morris Lapidus had been working diligently and productively. He had been paying out and paying out, waiting on faith for the hotel to charge forth. This delay was pushing Lapidus in one direction, financial ruin. In his distressed situation, he pled with the partners of the Fontainebleau, including Ben Novack, to reimburse at least his expenses. The reply was not what Lapidus was hoping for; he was referred to the hotel's lawyer. The lawyer liked Lapidus and his straight shooting honestly. He offered to hold a mock trial with the partners and Lapidus. In this meeting Morris Lapidus represented himself, used his former acting training and debate team skills, and presented his case thoroughly. His original response from the lawyer was not too hopeful. "The attorney confirmed the legal status of the partnership, namely, there was, in fact, no partnership, simply an understanding." (Lapidus 1979, 140) After the mock trial, Lapidus was assured by the lawyer that he would have the partners pay him his money.

Financial ruin was evaded by Morris Lapidus. Unfortunately for Lapidus, this was not going to be his only visit to financial distress during Fontainebleau construction.

Years after completed construction the **truth on The Fontainebleau name** came to light on February 23, 1957, when Ben Novack was quoted in *The Saturday Evening Post.* He said he came upon the title when he and his wife were vacationing in Europe and they saw the **Fontainebleau Palace in Fontainebleau, France**. The palace, Chateau de Fontainebleau, is a castle of sizable stature that makes a lasting impression.

This **Royal Chateau of Fontainebleau** remains one of the most fabulous castles of all time. It was built in a 49,000-acre forest as a **royal hunting lodge**. Lodge is a major understatement as the size of the castle is one where the room count continues for days. A town grew up around the castle and the chateau and town have worked symbiotically ever since. Located forty miles south of Paris, the palace is breathtaking. The chateau is brimming with gilded imperial furniture in neoclassical style, silk wall coverings and tapestries embellish the walls while decorative plasterwork fills every room and hallway with elegant adornment. King Louis VII, Philip Augustus, Louis IX, King Henri II, King Henri IV, and Emperor Napoleon Bonaparte all graced the chateau with their presence and appreciated it as a location of tranquility and grandeur. Napoleon gave the chateau his highest praise, making the chateau his primary residence and restored the palace to a finer quality after it had fallen to decline over time. Philip the Fair, Henry II, and Louis XIII took their first breaths of life in the great chateau.

The chateau is rich in history and is used today as a tourist destination, usually as a day trip from Paris. Peacocks freely roam the vast expanse of noble gardens while The Royal Chateau of Fontainebleau entertains visitors with pomp and grandeur.

As it turns out, Ben Novack wasn't the first guy with the idea. On November 8, 1961, the *Miami Herald* printed a piece saying, "Charles Kramer, president of the DiLido Hotel, was looking through old office files when he came across an architectural rendering of the diLido, [sic] which was built in 1953. The name on the drawing was 'Fontainebleau.' Kramer says he checked back and found that the original owners of the diLido [sic] had considered Fontainebleau as the name, but 'finally decided it was too long to remember'."

Chateau de Fontainebleau was a famous castle and many people knew the name. Many visitors graced the entryway of the castle. Ben Novack made the trip to the castle but was not one of these tourist visitors. He was quoted in that *Saturday Evening Post* article, "We didn't stop to look at it. I don't go for those foreign chateaux." To Novack, the name was catchy so he borrowed the title.

The name was not all Novack held dear upon his return. He informed Morris Lapidus that the internal design was to now be done in a **French Provincial** style. This was a bit of a curve ball to Lapidus as French Provincial was not a match at all to the grand modern hotel he was designing. As a matter of fact, French Provincial was exactly opposite to the hotel's style. French Provincial was a stately, formal style famous for balance and symmetry. Brick and stucco was often accented with copper and slate. The high hip roof was steep and prominent. Second story windows were over-tall and cut into the roofline with curved arches accenting their length. The entry was equally balanced on both sides of the structure with equal windows and equal chimneys.

Morris Lapidus was thoughtful when he collected a sampling of ideas for Ben Novack to preview. "This handsome style was perfect for small chateaux and country homes, but would be utterly ridiculous in a tropical contemporary luxury hotel." (Lapidus 1979, 143)

Thankfully for Morris, his sampling was well received and realized his hopeful intentions. "He took one look at the illustrations and wanted to know if I were crazy. I wouldn't have these old-fashioned interiors on a bet. I want that modern kind of French Provincial." (Lapidus 1979, 141) In reality, that didn't exist, so Morris Lapidus did what he did best. He designed what he wanted to design and sold it to Ben Novack as "that modern kind of French Provincial" that Novack desired.

This solution was one Lapidus was using on a regular basis with Ben Novack. He made the columns float by taking them directly through the ceiling in illuminated disappearing holes. He avoided heavy ornamentation of the tops and bottoms of columns and instead made them dominate with simplicity and clean lines. He introduced elegance with Old Vienna, Dresden figurines, rococo arches, gas lit crystal chandeliers, and Old World luxury.

Elaborate French Provincial was a bold statement. *Courtesy of Fontainebleau.*

Chapter 6
Architectural Skill

Morris Lapidus used the same technique he used in designing storefronts. He studied what people wanted and then designed to their desires. For this reason he made moments of staged "showcases" throughout the hotel. He knew people wanted to be noticed, to have their three seconds in the spotlight, and to soak in the applause. This is why he designed the famed Staircase to Nowhere, the sweeping outside staircases from the cabanas to the pool deck, and the mini landings throughout the hotel. This concept was recreated with the total remodel done by Fontainebleau Resorts in 2007.

Mr. Lapidus made a specific moment to shine on stage in a place where he thought for sure people would comment and complain about the oddity. When customers crossed over into the dining area of the restaurant he had them go up three stairs, take two steps and go down three stairs. When each guest was atop that landing for that moment they were on stage, the **Lapidus Landing** stage. The lights in that region were pink, allowing the customer's tan to glow. In addition to the spotlights, they were center stage for that moment. Lapidus commented on the landing by saying, "I have been waiting through the years for someone to tell me how ridiculous I was to arrange for guests to walk up three steps and then down three steps into the dining room when they could have walked directly in. I have a reply, but no one has ever asked me why: everyone loves a dramatic entrance." (Lapidus 1996, 164)

The now famous **Staircase to Nowhere** amplified this concept. In the main area of the Fontainebleau, Lapidus designed a staircase that had one real purpose, the ability to make an entrance. It was, however, disguised as a coat check. A traditionally thinking individual wouldn't consider a coat check in Miami were summer is the main cash crop but Lapidus wasn't traditional. He made the coat check specifically for a moment of glamour. When guests visited the Fontainebleau, they were dressed in their best clothes, wearing their most glamorous shoes and glistening with their finest jewelry. More importantly they donned their best wraps and fur stoles, summer or not. A trip up the stairs required a trip down the stairs, where each guest was in the spotlight looking down on all the "peasants." Guests staying at the hotel exited the elevator on the mezzanine level for the sole purpose of descending the staircase.

The "staircase to nowhere" was so named after years of popular use. *Courtesy of Fontainebleau.*

It was the moment was see and be seen. Lapidus said, "People love to ascend or descend circular staircases in a grand manner." (Lapidus 1996, 164) It gave the vacationer a personal moment in the sun as a glamorous human being. It produced a moment of dramatic entrance. All the while the other guests were looking up at the descending procession of class. The staircase was a subconscious moment to shine. It was like receiving an award for dressing up for the night. After it was built and the guests enjoyed the project, Lapidus watched the responses and got a chuckle, amazed that people got such a thrill out of nothing. They loved it!

Later in life, the Fontainebleau was blessed with a dedicated employee, Lisa Cole. As the Director of Public Relations for twenty-six years at the Fontainebleau, Cole called up Morris Lapidus from her job and said, "I would love to spend some time with you." Lapidus was thrilled with the phone call. He was well into his final years and the praise was appreciated.

Cole said, "I would go and pick (Morris Lapidus) up by limousine and bring him to the Fontainebleau for lunch and have him tell me stories. He was amazing. I tried to pull out what was sexy about the hotel. He wanted people to make an entrance – very grand but very subtle. The staircase Morris built for an entrance. He built it with a landing to do a pivot."

When the hotel was preparing for internal completion, Morris Lapidus sent one of his young architects down on the airplane to show Ben Novack the internal designs they had agreed to develop. When Novack saw the kid's papers, he hit the ceiling with rage. It was nothing like he desired. Immediately Morris Lapidus jumped a plane with copies of the internal designs and worked out his words the whole way to Miami. "I pointed out the rococo arches, the oversized Dresden figurines, the gay romantic Viennese pavilion over the quick service counter, the pseudo gaslight fixtures dripping with crystals." (Lapidus, 1996, 166) Ben Novack agreed with Morris Lapidus. Those were the proper plans to follow. Ironically, they were exactly the same plans Lapidus sent with his young architect only hours before.

Lapidus' design was interrupted during the construction of the hotel when he received a phone call one morning at 4 a.m. **A bomb** had gone off at the construction site. "Fortunately, the dynamiters had set their charges against one of the columns that supported a part of a two-story wing. The continuity of the hurricane-proof type of concrete construction kept the wing from collapsing." (Lapidus, 1979, 151)

With calculated precision and steady, consistent effort, more reinforcement was added and more concrete was poured. The incident was left as a questionable assurance as no disgruntled employee was encountered and no business disputes were present. Weeks after news of the bombing died down, Morris Lapidus happened upon a conversation with an employee with labor and gambling. The incident was put to rest in his mind with the one conversation. "Many of these fringe characters winter in Miami Beach. I recall saying that it was fortunate that whoever had set the bomb knew so very little about construction."

"Mr. Lapidus, these people know their business. Why should they try to destroy the hotel? **They just wanted to get a message across** – that's all they wanted." (Lapidus, 1979, 151)

When the construction was nearing completion, Morris Lapidus finalized the last details. Lapidus took his glamorous taste for style and went shopping. This is the same man that once designed a bathtub for the Vanderbilt mansion and upon seeing the bathtub Vanderbilt said, "I am not a Rockefeller, I can't afford that bath." (Desilets 2004, 73) With that same seasoning of extravagance, Morris Lapidus had a **$100,000 budget** to spend on elaborate furnishings and accents. He shopped on Third Avenue in New York, the antique district of the time, and chose the items he felt would best glamorize the hotel. In amongst various items he chose were numerous flying wooden angels. He knew they wouldn't fit in their current state but he wanted to upgrade them with gold plating and make them into lighting fixtures. His creation, in the long run, turned out to be a breathtaking accent of exquisite angels flanking the elevators and surrounding the lobby. After his laborious choosing of a grand piano, busts made of marble, elaborate clocks, decorative ornate lamps, and gilded cherubs to name a sampling, Lapidus had the items loaded up on a moving truck and shipped to Miami Beach. When the truck arrived, Lapidus received a high volume unhappy phone call from Ben Novack. Apparently someone sent a truck full of junk to the hotel and Novack was not too happy about the incident. Morris Lapidus immediately realized the items needed a more thorough introduction to Ben Novack, one that fully described the valuable qualities of the antique adornments.

Upon arrival in Miami Beach, Morris Lapidus met a content and happy Novack. Confused at the change in mood regarding the items, Novack apologized for his explosion over the phone. It turned out that, following the phone call, Ben Novack had taken a well-traveled, prominent couple on a tour of the hotel the night before Lapidus' arrival. Once the couple saw some of the items shipped on the truck that day, they were in awe at the beautiful pieces intended to adorn the hotel. Their reaction and educated knowledge of the valuable and rare pieces quickly changed Ben Novack's feelings about the items.

that just arrived by truck the previous day. They were standing on the furniture to reach high places and even using the marble busts as sawhorses for cutting wood and work table props. Ben Novack was irate, and rightly so, but if you ask a local, the workmen were confused because these were the very same items Novack was causing a "junk ruckus" about the day before.

One of the prized possessions chosen from Lapidus' shopping spree was a **statue from the Normandie ocean liner**. The statue was recovered from a bronze heap and purchased for $1,200. (Desilets 2004, 9) She was given the name **Lady Normandie Statue,** fixed up, and refinished with a white, clean exterior and positioned in front of the hotel entrance by a subtle low lying water fall. Lady Normandie has greeted thousands of guests as the years passed. The *S.S. Normandie* was a French ocean liner that broke numerous records, including the record for the largest and fastest oceangoing vessel known to the world in 1932, the year she was christened and launched.

At her launch on October 29, 1932, just over 200,000 onlookers were present. As the biggest ship at the time, with a hull of 27,567 tons, her launch created an unexpected result. As she sat in the water, her enormous size created an enormous wave that, yes, crashed into hundreds of spectators. Oddly, no one seemed to factor in

Sweeping design was audacious and brave in conservative 1954. *Courtesy of Fontainebleau.*

the concept that 27,567 tons would displace water. Thankfully no one was seriously hurt.

At the time of construction, the *S.S. Normandie* was part of a mad race involving ship builders. With the introduction of Prohibition, many large passenger ships were being built to accommodate passengers eager to get liquored up on the high seas. This was indeed *Normandie's* purpose in life.

In 1942 the ocean liner was transformed into a troopship. Sadly she caught fire and sank at Pier

He told Lapidus that the prior day was one filled with one major trauma after another and the truck took him by surprise. He was apologetic for his response but again hit the roof when he was carrying out his work on the hotel grounds the next day. The carpenters and workmen were committing blasphemy. They were destroying the priceless pieces

88 at the New York Passenger Ship Terminal. After forty-four years she was salvaged and sold off as scrap. According to Wikipedia, "She maintains the distinction of being the most powerful steam turbo-electric propelled passenger ship ever built."

The white statue is one of many now famous items salvaged from the great ship. In 2004, Lady Normandie was estimated to be worth $1.2 million.

The Lady Normandie Statue greeted 1954's guests as they drove up to the chateau.

The statue was well lit at night and surrounded by bubbling water and waterfalls.

Morris Lapidus didn't choose flamboyant, extravagant fixtures to sooth the customers. He chose them to glitz up the place, to make the guests feel like celebrities, and to add a feeling of extravagance. He himself called the items excessive rubbish, but he chose them because the public loved them. He said, "Why be exotic in private?" (Desilets 2004, 9)

Lapdius told Lisa Cole, Fontainebleau Director of Public Relations for twenty-six years during the years when Stephen Muss ran the hotel, more about his retrieval of items. "Morris had the chandeliers created," Cole said. These are the same famous chandeliers that were known worldwide. When Lapidus designed the hotel he had the whole package in mind. He knew his plan required large, ornate, but delicate chandeliers. In addition to his trips to New York City, Lapidus went to Belgium. He brought back twenty-seven train cars filled with priceless objects to further fill the hotel. The specific purpose of the trip was for obtain chandeliers.

Cole said, "I remember him telling me he couldn't find them so he had to make them. He had them designed and made in Belgium. For all three chandeliers it was $250,000 back then. There were 1,800 pieces of crystal in each one. They had to hand wash them on a ladder. It took three days." Each chandelier was roughly the size of a VW Bug with an eight-foot wide girth and a ten-foot depth.

The cleaning was a show in and of itself. Once a year the chandelier specialist would come and set up scaffolding in the lobby. From 11:30 p.m. to roughly 5:00 a.m., when the foot traffic was at its lowest, he would take down each crystal, wash it by hand and hang it back up again.

Lapidus used twenty-seven different colors of paint to adorn the walls. He followed his tried and true tactics to subconsciously entertain and enthrall visitors. He attracted them with light, what he called "The Moth Complex." He used constantly changing floor levels to create intrigue and mystery. One of Morris Lapidus' unspoken agendas was to bring out the inner child in vacationing adults, a subconscious desire of the visitors.

The hotel was nearly ready. Just prior to the big day, Ben Novack took a group of the investors and a few businessmen for a tour of the grounds. Little did he know, this was the day he nearly died, and it came at the hand of his own hard-working architect.

As already discussed, Morris Lapidus and Ben Novack had a working relationship that was trying and often conflicted. Evidence of this working tension was clearly visible the day **Lapidus nearly killed Novack over $40,000.**

As the story goes, Morris Lapidus had reached his breaking point. He was on the verge of bankruptcy for the second time in one year due to the Fontainebleau and the lack of Ben Novack paying Lapidus' bill. Morris Lapidus was using his life's savings to paying his own employee's salaries. He had put in endless hours of hard, dedicated work for mere pennies on the hour. Lapidus and Novack had discussed this matter on several occasions and Novack was very tardy with the money owed. An agreement had been made with Novack to compensate Lapidus enough to break even and avoid bankruptcy. On this tour around the grounds, Novack went to talk to Lapidus on several occasions but didn't cover the subject of the money as previously agreed. Ben Novack had talked to the investors, yet said nothing to Lapidus. With every single step they took around the property, the easy going Morris Lapidus grew more and more irate. He needed the cash that Novack had agreed to pay him. Novack wasn't following through on his end of the bargain and Lapidus was fuming.

Morris Lapidus brought up the topic and received the most unexpected response he had ever received. Ben Novack just stood there staring at him with a blank look of confusion. He was claiming he had no idea about any agreement.

Morris Lapidus exploded.

Literally.

He grabbed a timber off the pool deck and shot off after Ben Novack. Morris Lapidus had an agenda and Ben Novack read that agenda in his eyes. Novack ran the other direction and Lapidus chased him with the focus of a laser. The investors were baffled but thankfully defused the situation by tackling Lapidus. On the couch in the offices moments later, Lapidus explained the dire situation to the investors. They went to Novack, who was tucked away in his private office, to clear up the discrepancy. Novack wanted an apology and that was the only way he was coming out of his office as he said he feared for his own life. Morris Lapidus gave Novack his requested apology, and received an odd reply from Novack. According to Morris Lapidus, Ben Novack told him, "You should be sorry. Why didn't you talk louder? I never said I wasn't going to pay you. I didn't know what you were screaming about. You were whispering, and you know that I don't hear well." (Lapidus 1996, 171)

It was a well known fact that Ben Novack wore a hearing aid. He was often heard yelling as a result of his hearing challenge. Morris Lapidus admitted in the same telling of the story, "It was possible that, in fact, he had not heard me. I wish I could relive that awful moment and see whether or not I was wrong."

Regardless, Morris Lapidus was paid in notes on the spot.

Morris Lapidus said, "Why be exotic in private?" *Courtesy of Fontainebleau.*

Chapter 7
The Chateau Debut

In the end, the cost for the **550-room grand luxury hotel** was a whopping **$20 million**. Ben Novack's French princess was about to make her debut. The way Novack talked of her was consistent and very raw, his term **"Fountain Blue"** set a precedent and stuck as Novack held no pomp. Employees showed no care to put a French swing on the pronunciation as Novack showed no concern over the matter.

Fontainebleau was ready for customers and beaming. Her size for the time was gigantic. The lobby alone was 17,000 square feet. Contractors used 140 miles of electrical wire and 100 miles of pipes. Connections were made through 2,000 phone lines. The kitchen had a coffee urn that could make 250 gallons of coffee at one time. The dishes were pulled through a conveyer belt – an unheard of contraption at the time – to wash in an industrial washer.

Carpeting was a peculiar puzzle. The curve of the building created a certain amount of waste, as nothing was square. The turning hallway made for a more secluded feeling for the guest, as you couldn't see strait down the tunnel hallway; the curve blocked your view and made it feel more private. Rolling out the carpet and adjusting for the sweeping curve in the hallways, however, created an adventure in carpet mathematics. The rooms were not as bad as the hallway, but still the curving walls made for an over-estimation in numbers at the widest part of the room. Taking all this into account, twenty-five acres of carpeting covered the floors. Light fixtures were filled with 8,000 light bulbs. An air-conditioning system consisting of 13,000 tons was set to cool. The ballroom was originally planned to hold 9,000 people and stand as a casino but the finished result was still a glamorous, breathtaking area. The best aspect of all was probably the guest to staff ratio with one and a half workers per guest. The staff was made up of 847 well-trained individuals who were held to a strict dress code. The outfits were impeccable, with extra coats and ties hanging in their lockers as back up relief if ever there was a stain. Personnel included fourteen policemen and forty-five telephone operators. Even a furniture repair shop was situated in the basement, ready for action.

Outside the grounds were covered with elaborate gardens, fountains, and statues. Four quadrants of maze-like patterned bushes and foliage puzzles created a visual garden quilt. The oversized pool was the central attraction, but also acted as an accent to the gardens, cabanas, and ocean. The underbelly of the pool was visible through large windows at the dining patio off the dining room. This dining patio was a good place to find teenage boys, specifically near the windows.

The north edge of the pool was the focal point with the visual focus on diving boards, a hotel pastime long lost to the land of lawsuits. Two competition worthy springboards flanked a towering diving platform. The top concrete diving stage rose up over seven stories into the air and towered over the two story cabanas. Both platforms had their own springboard and were connected by twenty-three ascending stairs. The underbelly of the pool was filled with viewing windows, allowing guests inside the hotel to watch the swimmers from below the surface.

The cabanas wound in arching curves, multiple stories stacked upon each other giving a grand total of 250 units. The units made up a winding and curving serpentine structure that ranged from one to three levels depending on the location. Access to the second and third floors could be made through the cabana elevator, yes, a cabana elevator. Cabana units filled both sides of the serpentine structure, allowing guests to either face the pool or the ocean. Winding open staircases connected to the concrete floor allowing guests an alternative to the elevator. This was all part of architect Morris Lapidus' plan as it was another descending moment in the limelight. The concept was only amplified when you added beautiful women in culturally disappearing swimsuits. The bikini had only been around for a handful of years and the appearance of skin at the pool was becoming enormously popular.

Opposite page:
Poolside diving boards are an aspect of the past nationwide due to insurance and lawsuits.

The biggest marker for the year was air conditioning. This creature comfort was hitting beach establishments with praise. Movie theaters were the first location to fully utilize the cool luxury of air-conditioning; hotels followed as they could afford. The DiLido and the Ritz near Lincoln Road were written up in the local paper for their recent addition of AC at the time the Fontainebleau was being built.

The whole establishment went through a **feverish dry run** to make sure beds were all washed and remade, enough towels were ready and waiting, food was cooked properly and in synchronicity with the wait staff. Ovens were tested for appropriate temperature, dishes were cooked and re-cooked, maids were bustling, and bellhops were rhythmically flowing to the tune of a humming hotel.

The much awaited hotel opening was christened with a **Grand Ball that Christmas in 1954**. The ball was to benefit two local hospitals, Mt. Sinai and St. Francis. Starting their first day on a philanthropy ticket was good press. The ball was held on Monday, December 20, for $50 per person. A grand total of 1,600 guests made reservations for the great event while over 300 people were turned away for lack of available space. The dinner brought in $80,000, all of which was reported in the *Miami Herald* as donated funds to the hospitals. Guests all wore elegant evening attire complete with fine jewels and gloved hands. French décor dripped from the ceilings and walls and festooned the floors and the wait staff answered promptly when called *garcon*. The weather was oddly cool, creating a brisk evening perfect for showing off your finest fur coat. The moon was full and the sky was clear. The *Miami Herald* quoted one guest as saying, "You can't get in, you can't get a drink, you can't get anything, but isn't this the grandest hotel you ever saw?"

Another guest said, "Everything was big – the number of guests, the size of the diamonds, the lusciousness of the furs. To say nothing of the hotel itself – you'll have to visit it many times before you can take it all in, it's so tremendous." (Woodward 1954)

An additional visitor said, "Yes, it was a fantastic evening, it was just like a movie with ten reels going at once." (Woodward 1954)

The guests dined on "French-ish" cuisine. First they ate les marveleux délices `a la Fontainebleau, which was really a portion of lox, smoked sturgeon, and caviar. Next they indulged in L' Elixir Gastronomes `a la Impériale, which was really beef soup. The main course followed, serving up a delectable poitrine de bolaille Fontainebleau, haricots verts fraîches, et pommes château rissole, which was really chicken, green beans, and potatoes. The dessert capped off the meal with a fabulous production of La Rosèe Poètiques Gourmandises Le Plaisir d'Empire, which was actually a macaroon accompanying praline ice cream. Café de prince, Turkish coffee, was served with the desert. The night was a wonderful success. The hotel officially opened the next day.

Morris Lapidus was present, watching his customers enjoy his creation. Ben Novack was present, equipped and ready for business. Prominent locals were there to enjoy the grandeur as well as celebrity faces ready to enjoy a luxurious Christmas.

Congratulations and praise were both lavishly spread on the builder and architect. The groundbreaking design was a success. The luxurious décor was well received by guests. The staged moments in the spotlight were drunk in and absorbed. Business was booming and smiles were beaming. All the hard work, lost sleep, and stress produced the most luxurious and grand hotel of all time.

The Grand Opening Ball had one carefully chosen visitor, **Homer Pajot**, the mayor of the town of Fontainebleau, France. Ben Novack thought it would be a good addition to the new hotel. Pajot came with a beautiful tree from the very forest that surrounded the Chateau Fontainebleau, the castle from where the Fontainebleau gained its name. The Chateau was a famous hunting lodge built for royalty in the deep thick forest of France. This made the tree an appropriate grand opening gift. That was until the U.S. Customs Department in the airport saw the tree. They confiscated the sapling, leaving Mayor Pajot empty handed.

The Frenchmen moved to Plan B. They had a tree delivered from The Exotic Gardens on Lincoln Road. This is the very same Exotic Gardens that Miami Beach developer Carl Fisher **bent the law** to build when he quickly and efficiently erected the building so that the protesters couldn't afford to cover the cost of removal. The building now stands as a beloved Italian restaurant, Carnevale. The presentation of the French forest sapling would have been a grand success if a journalist had not seen the delivery truck making the hand-off. Regardless, the Exotic Gardens tree was planted in the grand Fontainebleau garden replicating the *petit jardins* from Versailles. A plaque brought from France was presented to Ben Novack and displayed in the gardens. The plaque read: May the sun warm your day and the moon and the stars bring happy evenings.

Mayor Pajot was a bit bewildered by the hotel. It didn't match the Louis XIV Palace and the Napoleon Palace to which he was accustomed. The scale was not close in comparison, the curve had nothing to do with the French Chateau, the décor wasn't really in the same ballpark of the castle, and the ocean was a different backdrop than the lush French forest of Fontainebleau. The reaction from the prestigious French guest was not complementary. He called it "*C'est une bouillabaisse*," a Mediterranean fish stew. This stew is generally accepted as a topic for heated discussion and criticism. Like many dishes, it takes effort to make it tasteful. In America our equivalent contender is "Musgo," that is everything in the refrigerator that must go, cooked together as a collective vegetable soup. *C'est une bouillabaisse* is the must go version from the fish docks. All the unworthy for sale or unsold fish is added to a cackle of seasonings and plethora of spices. Usually this soup is sold to the hard working, little paid dockworkers.

Clearly the French mayor's response to the hotel was left questionable. Morris Lapidus had a smattering of the French language in his resume of talents and inquired on the mayor's comment. The response by the Mayor Pajot was that he liked this soup but only on a rare occasion.

As most life changing events go, the opening of the Fontainebleau was not all blubbering praise. In fact, it was far from it as it was filled with **uninhibited and highly vocal critics.**

Along with the prominent visitors came reporters, local journalists, and writers from prominent architectural magazines and national publications.

Life Magazine called Morris Lapidus a controversial architect. The style of design received a mocking jab when the magazine said Lapidus turned Miami Beach French.

Architectural Forum informed Lapidus that they would not be submitting a piece on the Fontainebleau because, "it was too controversial, that it violated all the precepts of building design." The editor called Lapidus personally and said, "Morris, what the hell did you do? You've created a monstrosity. I'd lose my job if I published this thing." This gave Morris Lapidus a vivid understanding of how different his designs were to the then current standard.

Progressive Architecture said, "they could not publish such a radical piece of work."

Architectural Record told him, "The Fontainebleau was too far off the mainstream of architecture to warrant publication."

The *New York Times Magazine* described the hotel as, "An extension of the carnival midway in concrete, lighted up at night like the entrance to the Tunnel of Love. The total effect is not un-engaging, the impression of luxury is not false; the mixing and mingling of motifs is likely to amuse the worldly, enrage the purist, and overwhelm the uninitiated; the food is fine, and only the snob could complain." (Millstein 1957)

The critics thought the Fontainebleau design was noisy and overdone. The décor in 1954 was modest, not celebratory as Morris Lapidus designed.

Morris Lapidus responded by telling publications that he designed for the wild and celebratory outing, not the mundane and steady consistency of home. He wanted visitors to have a lively time, one that was like no other. He told the *New York Times*, "It's the crazy hat for a woman, the bright tie for men."

It was published that Morris Lapidus was architecture's Frank Lloyd Wrong. Some writers wrote that his style was vulgar and others said he had gone mad. Literally. Overall he was criticized as too much.

Frank Lloyd Wright himself had a comment or two about Lapidus' style. "Wright once compared the Fontainebleau to an anthill." (Hanks 2005)

The New York Times commented with distaste on his style of "super schlock." The famous *Times* architecture critic Ada Louise Huxtable was unforgivably vile in some of her statements. She said, "One man's joy is another man's Hell. I never felt so joyless than in the midst of all that joy. I was depressed in the direct ratio of aesthetic literacy and hokey pretensions to the shoddiness of the execution. I got a terrible case of the Fontana blues."

The critics were relentless and his peers were vocal with their opinions. Morris Lapidus broke the rules of architecture and his work was highly misunderstood in the design world. The '50s were a conservative time. This was a wild move.

The American Institute of Architecture suspended Morris Lapidus after the Fontainebleau opened for business.

For the general public, the actual consumers of Lapidus' work, it was a different story. They loved his designs. They ate up his planned, staged moments. They socialized, entertained, and, most importantly, they booked their next trip. Encouraging customers to come back again is the surest sign and most significant trait of a truly successful hotel.

Morris Lapidus heard the critics and he heard them clearly. His attitude was confident, yet hurt. His response was, "People need something to give them a lift. I'm selling them a hotel, a luxurious, playful atmosphere. There's nothing else to sell." He knew he provided a service to the subconscious. He said, "My hotels are to tickle, to amuse." (Lapidus 1996, 174)

Lapidus was not the type of person to ignore the comments that came his way. Often times, when people get criticized they don't read the potentially hurtful print. Lapidus didn't play by that method. He said, "I was torturing myself more every time I read some pipsqueak critic's comments: 'garish' – 'vulgar' – 'pandering to the nouveau rich' – 'a talented architect who has sold out to achieve notoriety'." (Lapidus 1996, 174)

Still he stood by his plans. After many years he admitted, "I was not going to be worried by what the critics said. Oh yes, I might be hurt by what they would say about my work, and I was." He was well off the norm of traditional design so it really was no jolt that he rocked the architectural world. He changed everything about building style and design. He continued, "Regardless of whether the critics like it or not, I would continue doing things my way, just as long as I was true to my own convictions and could continue to please at least the public, because people were my chief interest. If I could please people, then I knew that I was doing the right thing." (Lapidus 1996, 174)

The Fontainebleau filled with luxurious furniture, extravagant wall prints, lights, fountains, and marble busts was a breath of fresh air breaking the every day cycle of regular life. In the Fontainebleau, Conservative kicked off her shoes, spun in circles with her arms flung wide, and basked in the limelight of *show time.*

Morris Lapidus was a survivor and a diligent man. He heard the critics and it affected him greatly. As tough as the hard words were to swallow, he stepped up to the plate. **Lapidus focused on his customers not his critics**.

Lapidus designed the hotel specifically angled at what the people wanted. Free flowing curved areas filled the hotel because he knew people liked to explore and float through spaces. The whole building was designed around making people feel good. Lapidus determined he was selling a product when designing the hotel and that product was a good time.

At the time, hotels in America were not architectural wonders, instead they were places to sleep. A handful of hotels across the nation were exciting Art Deco style dreams but nothing compared to the scale of the Fontainebleau. There was no competition. The Fontainebleau was the first hotel to provide a whole package including rooms, glamorous decorations, entertainment, shopping, activities, swimming pools, and the ocean. Traditional hotels throughout the country were nowhere near 550 rooms in size and provided one thing, a place to sleep with the possibility of a gift shop.

Chapter 8
Fully Functioning Fontainebleau

The Fontainebleau was a swinging establishment filled with smiles and good times. The cabanas were fit accents for laughing kids, card playing ladies, gambling men, summering locals, and were even used as guestrooms when the hotel was maxed to capacity.

In 1954 Fontainebleau wasn't only the best hotel in Miami Beach, it was the best hotel in the world.

The hotel filled business needs with a stock exchange where the tickertape ran at poolside. Shops filled the interior, providing everything from a book to lingerie. A jewelry store and a hair salon were accented with dress shops and accessories stores.

In the early years of ownership, Ben Novack was pumping his money back into the Fontainebleau. This changed as the years ticked on, but initially the coin was free flowing on the Fontainebleau grounds. Card games, canasta, mahjong, or gin rummy were played poolside and the 250 cabanas were usually filled with business deals and personal transactions while husbands were away on business trips. Some cabanas were so far away from the pool that it was a mile walk there and back.

Inside the hotel, the **Poodle Lounge** served *hors d'oeuvres* for free while men sat and enjoyed a cocktail before dinner. Most women didn't frequent the Poodle Lounge as the place was stocked with upscale hookers who rented their stools from the bartender. These were freelancing ladies, not employees or ladies connected to the hotel. A better stool could cost you $200 a night. An unknowing woman was often known to sit at the bar only to be told by the bartender, "Miss, it'll cost you to sit in that one." Some of the hookers allowed themselves to serve their customers with pleasant conversation as a dinner date while others were full service oriented ladies. One lady was specifically known as the Madame of the Fontainebleau, and didn't leave until the property was closed for reconstruction in early 2006. Alice was in her later years, some say early eighties and still cared enough to dress in her full glamour with her elegant high, high heels, eye catching stockings, full make-up with bright red lipstick, and her hair done to perfection.

A traditional day at the Fontainebleau was filled with the pool or ocean in the morning then a late afternoon rest. Happy hour at the Poodle Lounge preceded a grand entrance down the **Staircase To Nowhere,** where everyone could see you make your performing entrance.

Maze patterns accented the formal gardens making the grounds inviting locations to explore.

The average Fontainebleau day is best described by Michael Aller. As one of the best assets to Miami Beach today, **Michael Aller** is **Tourism and Convention Director, Chief of Protocol.** "Mr. Miami Beach," Michael Aller, has privileged knowledge as he grew up in the Fontainebleau. Aller's father owned the company that supplied the marble for the Fontainebleau. From the famous black and white bow tie marble floor to the patio deck, Aller's father was the supplier. His business was as solid as the stones he provided. They quarried Italian marble or whatever material was needed from their multiple sites throughout the world. For Ben Novack, the solid hotelier known for his high volume solution to issues, Aller was a formidable, skilled man. When Novack couldn't pay the bill for the flooring, he discovered Aller was a qualified negotiator. Aller worked out a deal, agreeing to take the principle owed his company in the form of an apartment at the Fontainebleau and to collect the remainder from Novack over time.

The apartment ran the length of the Fontainebleau from the ocean to the bay. The over 3,000-square-foot, three-bedroom unit on the 12th floor was beautiful. As Novack owed the company well over a million dollars, the apartment was only partial reimbursement. Michael Aller was fifteen years old when they moved into the family's new home.

As most other kids throughout the country were struggling with

Michael Aller lived in the Fontainebleau alongside visiting celebrities.

feeling awkward in their puberty years and fighting the curse of acne, and gossip, Michael Aller was walking down the Fontainebleau corridors with Dean Martin … literally. The celebrities knew him and took him under their wings. He was always there, roaming the hotel every time the entertainment came to perform. Their consistent visits developed a relationship with the young boy growing up at the Fontainebleau. Michael would run up to Dean Martin and walk with him, hearing the consistent and comforting, "How you doin' kid?" This was in marked contrast to the normal elbow shrug received by the general population.

Michael Aller remembers those days with a sparkle in his eye and a smile on his lips, "I felt like Superman. It was Dean Martin! And he knew me!

Me!" His list of favorite celebrities runs like a gossip column, and that was his everyday life.

Aller remembered the grand times with pride. The hotel was filled with wealthy, highflying individuals as well as celebrities. This was no low budget hotel; this was where the people with money came to play. He remembered two specific gentlemen, jewelers, who came down from New York. "They would sell jewelry right out of their pockets at the hotel." Custom made jewelry was a normal sight at the Fontainebleau.

With all the great moments he lived, one of the best accomplishments, according to Aller, was his touring interview with Morris Lapidus, walking through the Fontainebleau. Michael heard the stories that made up the hotel's history straight from Lapidus.

This interview near the end of Lapidus' life was not only the recounting of a lifetime of memories; it was an honor for Michael Aller.

For Aller, everyday Fontainebleau encompassed his everyday activities. The nightly festivities were consistent and it always included the Staircase to Nowhere. Michael Aller remembered his dad going to the Poodle Lounge for a pre-dinner drink. He would then get a phone call from his wife on the house phone. She would tell him what jewelry to bring up from the safe. Young Aller would put on his coat and tie and the whole family would make their entrance down to dinner.

The lobby stairway was indeed a dedicated moment of display. It was common practice for the ladies to exit the elevator on the mezzanine level, where the coat check was located. They checked their fur wraps and gracefully took their moment in the spotlight gliding down the stairs to their dinner reservations.

Michael Aller remembers his mother always wore a glamorous gown with her fine jewels. When they took the elevator down to dinner, they exited the lift on the mezzanine floor for their moment in the limelight. His mother and father always walked down together with Michael following behind, always behind. Aller remembered his mother beaming in her beautiful gown. Then at the bottom of the staircase she would always turn to Michael following behind her to ask a question or say something. "It meant nothing, of course, but it gave her a reason to turn around and show off the back of her gown."

Dinner at the **Fleur de Lys Room** was followed by a show in the La Ronde. Multiple nightclubs still existed on the beach and some guests left the hotel for outside entertainment but usually people settled back at the Fontainebleau to chat over the night's activities at **Chez Bon Bon** or outside in the garden. As this was the Fontainebleau, it wasn't just Mary and Joe, from New York, whom you met poolside the day before, but it was the normal guests at the hotel, which included Woody Allen, Milton Berle, Governor Kennedy, Marilyn Monroe, Henny Youngman, Sophie Tucker, and Arthur Miller to name a few. People would talk about who they saw and what they ate, but the atmosphere was always predictable, pleasing to the eye, and enjoyable.

The Fontainebleau was a step above any other location in the world. Everything was meant to dazzle and highlight elegance. Even the people who worked at the original Fontainebleau still comment on how they were treated, with quality and respect. The concept of calling a guest through an intercom was not considered, instead a message was delivered on a silver tray or a maitre d' in a dress coat and tie carried a handheld chalkboard with a message formally requesting the presence of the guest in need.

Employees at the hotel followed a high class dress code. Jacket and tie was standard issue with extra pressed versions of the same waiting in lockers in case of a sudden stain.

The black bow tie marble flooring in the lobby was polished every night. Employees dusted when they wouldn't be seen. Guests were greeted with a smile and overall the service was pristine.

Before the Fontainebleau, it was illegal to have retail shops or a nightclub in a hotel. Ben Novack changed that. People came to see people. People came to dine. People came to drink. People came to be part of something.

The Fontainebleau was brilliant business as it funneled visitors to areas of interest like the Boom Boom Room bar, the Chez Bon Bon Coffee Shop, the La Ronde Room for a show, or the Fleur de Lys dining room. Novack didn't want people in the grand entry just sitting around, he wanted them to live!, to spend!, to make a moment!

Fontainebleau's success became so great that it again changed the face of Miami Beach. The attendance at the local storefronts and nightclubs dwindled. Many nearby shop owners were forced out of business because of the success of the Fontainebleau.

The grand opening of the Fontainebleau carried an electric buzz for many years thereafter. The hotel was dynamic and swept the scene with style and grace; glamour was extravagance at a time when conservative was the norm.

Many people looked forward to the energy the Fontainebleau was creating. As they built the hotel, the spark was igniting a dwindling fire of beach enthusiasm.

In 1954, a postage stamp cost 3 cents, the minimum wage was 75 cents an hour, and the average income was $3,960 a year. A loaf of bread was 17 cents and a gallon of milk was 92 cents, but no one bought a gallon of milk at the store. Instead, the milkman left full bottles on your front doorstep at the same time he picked up the empties. The vast majority of women didn't work; instead they stayed home and kept a clean house, cooked healthy garden fresh meals, and clipped wet clothes to the laundry line in the backyard. The *Miami Herald* had a piece on a neighboring three bedroom, two bath home on DiLido Island that sold for $21,000 the very same month the Fontainebleau opened. Popular television shows were "Leave it to Beaver" and "I love Lucy." Children were disciplined for chewing gum in school and taking a drive was the family highlight for the week. The Fontainebleau changed the feeling of entertainment and the concept of vacation.

Chapter 9
The Eden Roc

For Morris Lapidus, the architectural world's praise was lacking but the visitors of the Fontainebleau loved what they saw. In addition to that, another call came to Lapidus. This time it was a request for a meeting with **Harry Mufson**, a former partner of Ben Novack's. Mufson was the same gentlemen in partnership with Novack at the Sans Souci Hotel. Yes, that partner, the one that sued Novack at the birth of the Fontainebleau's building process for allegedly using Sans Souci funds on the Fontainebleau. At the time of the lawsuit, Harry Mufson was requesting a divided share of the Fontainebleau. As it turned out, Morris Lapidus was told by Mufson that he bought the property directly north of the Fontainebleau and planned to build a grander, better hotel than the Fontainebleau.

To say Novack was pissed off with Morris Lapidus going to work for his former business partner was an understatement. From Lapidus' viewpoint, he was taking a job to further his career. After all, money is money and Lapidus had no problem working with Harry Mufson on the Sans Souci project. Mufson wasn't a dull man to work with, he was more reasonable than Novack, and was considered a breath of fresh air to Lapidus.

Ben Novack responded to the new partnership with resentment. He was livid with Morris Lapidus and Harry Mufson for going into business on the neighboring hotel. They were both banned from the Fontainebleau by Novack. However, Mufson was determined to see Lapidus' Fontainebleau creation, so he was left with little choice but to enter by stealth. He wanted to see what all the hoopla was all about, so he put on a disguise and walked right into the Fontainebleau. After his visit, Harry Mufson told Morris Lapidus, "I don't care if it's Baroque or Brooklyn. Just get me plenty of glamour and make sure it screams luxury. I want the Fontainebleau to fall flat on their ass." (Lapidus 1996, 192) The Fontainebleau opened in 1954, the Eden Roc in 1955.

Lapidus designed the hotel in modern Italian Renaissance style. Henry Mufson brought about the "American Plan" with the Eden Roc, and saw great success when one price bought everything you needed, including room and board. A hotel vacation became an all-inclusive stay. Immediately, other hotels adopted the program.

Morris Lapidus was pleased with the outcome of The Eden Roc. When he was designing the structure, he was going for the same grand style that he developed for the Fontainebleau but twisted it into a different flare, one that he referred to as a "cruise liner."

The Eden Roc was shaped like a Y after architect Morris Lapidus received horrible criticism for his flowing, curved Fontainebleau Chateau.

The criticism he received on the Fontainebleau was heavy and extreme. For this reason he changed his style and said, "The building and interiors I considered my best work. It wasn't as glamorous as the Fontainebleau, but it had an intimacy and gem-like beauty because it was so carefully detailed."

Elizabeth Taylor celebrated her birthday at the Eden Roc. She wasn't the only celebrity in residence;

Jane Mansfield brought together the union of marriage with her honeymoon at the Eden Roc. Desi Arnes and Lucille Ball were often there and Barbara Streisand sang there. Or did she? She was hired in 1961 to sing there, but less than ten people showed up for her show. She was asked by management to hold the show, but she could remain at the hotel as a vacation destination for herself. (Cohen 2002)

To the architectural community, Lapidus was still seen as controversial and risky but still he **billed $50 million over his architecture career.** After the Fontainebleau he was hired to build over 100 more buildings. Critics were uninhibited with their tongue lashings of his work but Lapidus didn't take it lying down. In his book *Too Much is Never Enough,* he said, "Less is more. How stupid can you be? Less is not more. Less is nothing."

The biggest success for the Eden Roc, known worldwide, is one aspect possessed by no one else. The funny thing is, this aspect, **The Spite Wall,** is not even on their grounds.

The rectangular Eden Roc was pulled to the curving Fontainebleau with the front overhang.

In Ben Novack's fury, he responded with a knee-jerk reaction. Ben Novack was a pressure cooker ready to burst. He was irate with Mufson for suing him, wasting his money, stalling the building of the Fontainebleau, and he was furious with Lapidus for going to work with the traitor Mufson. Morris Lapidus came to Novack, out of courtesy, and told him that he was being hired as the architect next door. Novack's response was an absolute **NO!** There was no negotiating and no compromise. Morris Lapidus was a reasonable man but was, in fact, living in America where he was free to work any project he chose. For Lapidus, he was taking a paying job.

This was not just a job; it was a much-needed job as he did the Novack job at such a preposterously low fee. He needed the money from another project. It's normal, everyday business practice to leave a job site and head to another job. Novack had no right to tell Lapidus how to run his business and he informed Novack that this was the case.

Lapidus shaped the building to replicate a Y. He placed a fountain in the shape of a gondola at the hotel entrance and set in it a replica of the *Winged Victory of Samothrace*, the headless statue of the Greek Goddess Nike representing victory. In addition, he designed the balconies to appear like loge boxes at an Italian opera.

Eden Roc was completed by Christmas in 1956. Lapidus was extremely popular with clients and customers, but remained extremely unpopular with his own architectural peers. Morris Lapidus tore up tradition with his new style. The public couldn't get enough; they salivated like dogs with each new project he designed. The Fontainebleau was really the start of the Lapidus saga, after which he was commissioned for project after project. The Eden Roc kept the momentum going as his career was launched into a strong, solid pace of steady work.

As construction was underway on the Eden Roc, Ben Novack went to the city and got approval for the plans of a new building to sit on the edge of the Fontainebleau property. This new building was to face south, and only south. Nothing was to face north. Somehow he got the city to approve his building with the north-facing wall consisting of a solid slab of dreary, bland concrete. This new building was an enormous expansion to the current Fontainebleau grounds for 1958.

The irritated and seething Novack called his former architect Morris Lapidus for the project as he wanted continuity on his own property. He said he wanted a flat wall to block the Eden Roc. Morris said no and wanted no part of the project.

The whole width of the property, was covered with one thing, **concrete.** A couple of pipes ran down the length of the building, but nothing else. Originally, Ben Novack **wanted to paint the wall black but that plan never came to fruition.** I'm sure it was a pleasure to Ben Novack to see those pipes rust in the salty air and make the view much worse than just the original, horrible, shadow-producing wall. The wall is a solid sea of ugly concrete – pasty, creamy, dull, monochromatic, concrete – seventeen stories tall.

The new building added 920 leisure rooms at the Fontainebleau.

Windows didn't exist on the wall, that is except for the windows at the top, the ones facing the panoramic view of the ocean. These windows were for the Novack residence and Ben Novack's personal office. Ben Novack left his suite of rooms in the main building with the grand curve and moved his family to a two story apartment in the new building where he could be closer to his new office. If you ask local Michael Aller, Ben Novack was known to open his office window just to spit on his neighbor's grounds.

The Eden Roc didn't take the building lightly. Eden Roc Hotel managing director, George Fox was very vocal and said it, "Placed our swimming pool in the shade and made guests feel like they were sitting in the Grand Canyon." (Donated press clipping)

Needless to say, Harry Mufson took Ben Novack to court.

Again.

The Spite Wall was a bland, ugly sea of nauseating concrete. The strip of windows at the top eastern side was Ben Novack's office and personal home.

The Eden Roc pool was swamped in shade by the beastly wall. *Courtesy of Sidney Mehr.*

The case was known as The Spite Wall Case. "The Eden Roc sued for 5 million dollars in damages, but the case was dismissed in Circuit Court." (Donated press clipping)

The result of the **lawsuit** was an acceptable price to pay for Novack. The judge ordered Ben Novack to pay for a new pool at the Eden Roc. This pool was built on the second floor of the Eden Roc grounds, just above the restaurant sitting right on the sand. It was over twenty years later that the boardwalk and dunes were built. The second pool was much smaller in comparison, but settled the dispute lawfully. To comply with the new pool, Harry Mufson needed to acquire variances from the city. It was not in the city books to build that close to the ocean.

Lisa Cole was told about the situation by Morris Lapidus. Cole said, "There have since been laws that you cannot build to affect someone else's sun line." (Oral Interview, 11/20/07)

Ever since that famous ugly wall has been called *The Spite Wall*. It has been written up in many published pieces, has changed laws in many states, and has been the source of many conversations by architectural enthusiasts worldwide.

The wall has caused some confusion to locals. Some thought The Spite Wall was a whole separate wall as another wall existed in the later years.

When Steven Muss took on the hotel in the late 1970s, he changed the pools and a wall. The six story 13,000-square-foot wall stood at the south end of the property. On this wall was a gorgeous **trompe l'oeil mural** of a stone pillar and an arched entryway. Behind the entryway were the hotel grounds, famous grotto pool and stone waterfall, hotel, and ocean. The concrete wall, with mural, covered nearly the whole block and pictured the building and the ocean that you'd be looking at… if you weren't looking at the mural of the building and the ocean.

This was not The Spite Wall.

The Spite Wall was built intentionally to ruin the Eden Roc's pool, which is the north wall of the Fontainebleau grounds, the mural was the South Wall. The mural was a beautiful picture. The Spite Wall was solid concrete with only a few windows adorning the wall at the top, ocean side, for Ben Novack's office. Surely he enjoyed many days at the office looking at his own handiwork: the shadow covering the pool. Spite, spite, spite, spite, spite. Ahhh … it made for a relaxing day at work for Novack. In 2007, the wall was tucked away as a new Eden Roc tower was built. The tower was much anticipated in the city as put a humorous, architec-

turally childish act to rest as well as adding to the city's room count and enabling larger conventions. The trompe l'oeil mural came down in November of 2002 to make room for the tower.

The Spite Wall was visible from the north for at least a mile away.

Ben Novack's home and office were behind the top windows that peered over the side wall.

Chapter 10
The Flourishing Years

The Fontainebleau was successful in the early years. Guests came from all over the world to experience the excitement and buzz that filled the air in the grandest hotel of all time. Guests included the full variety of people, from normal people on a traditional holiday vacations to high-end celebrities. Locals mingled with the high-end guests as they rented cabanas for the summer months. *Everyone* who was *anyone* was there and *everyone else* who wanted to *be someone* longed to be there. It didn't matter if you lived in Ohio or New York, when you were home leading your normal life, you thought about the Fontainebleau. When you picked up a magazine, you read about what was happening at the Fontainebleau. When you turned on the news, the entertainment clips covered the Fontainebleau.

Life happened at the Fontainebleau.

Local resident Laura Lauer recalled her days at the swanky hotel, "I wore stockings with the girdle, high, high heels and tight, tight dresses. The most uncomfortable get-ups you can imagine. Dresses so tight you had to yank them up to sit down. To pee was a major miracle." (Oral Interview, 9/3/07)

It has been published that the most famous Jewish mob man, **Meyer Lansky, was the most famous non-guest** of the Fontainebleau. Lansky was an infamous American Gangster along with his cohort and childhood friend, Charles "Lucky" Luciano. Together these two men were credited with the formation of the National Crime Syndicate in the United States. Lansky was known as the Godfather of Godfathers. As Al Capone was known for his bloody violence, Lansky was known as the thinking man's mob boss.

News in the papers and magazines across the nation was filled with Fontainebleau updates.

"Meyer Lansky was reckoned to be and was targeted by the U.S. Justice Department as, the biggest gangster in the United States – a dangerous lawbreaker of extraordinary power." (Lacey 1991, 10)

Meyer Lansky was known to use the Fontainebleau as his office and business center. He first lived at 612 Hibiscus Drive, Golden Isles, Hallandale, Florida, just a short clip up the beach. After a short jail stay he moved to 5255 Collins Avenue in the **Imperial House**. Newsmen and federal agents were often watching him as he walked his Shih Tziu named Bruiser along Collins Avenue.

Cheese holes, according to Morris Lapidus.

Architectural eye candy wasn't hard to find at the Fontainebleau.

The beach has always been known as a popular gangster location as business was not only prevalent, it was prosperous. The S&G Syndicate was well known here in the 1920s and business just grew from there. Lansky was reportedly earning $300 million a year. Hoteliers needed business and were reluctant to have mob men on the grounds regularly but at the same time were happy to accept their money. A cabana was rented for a steady $15,000 to $30,000 a year for bookie activity. Police officials were paid off and business was business. Surprise raids were made for several reasons, one being to appease journalists. It was a funny thing though; somehow it was a rare day when anyone was actually found in those surprise raids. They often resulted in nothing but wasted time. As the beach aged, the organized crime changed with the times and developed into working commerce. Al Capone took the opportunity of Prohibition to provide liquor.

Just prior to the years when the Fontainebleau was built, bookies in the area were estimated to spend $1 million in payoffs to buy immunity. Shortly thereafter, Tennessee Senator Estes Kefauver's **Congressional Crime Committee** was launched on May 3, 1950.

The house wasn't swept clean the first day thereafter. In 1969 Sunny Isles had a headline-hitting day when motels were being subpoenaed regarding a so-called "Mafia Summit." Meyer Lansky was actively in attendance. After the clean up was made and the city was no longer involved in active mobster business, believe it or not, the local law-abiding businessmen raised their voices. They saw a huge difference in their finances and wanted the business back. The local paper ran a story with the headline, "Return our hoodlums, merchants ask." (Stofik 2005, 48)

Lansky lived out his later years modestly in the Imperial House just north of the Fontainebleau by a few blocks. He was living a normal life in his elderly years, specifically trying to give the FBI no gravy for their research. *Miami Herald* reporter Hank Messick often followed Lansky looking for a story. His book was entitled *Syndicate in the Sun* in 1968 and today sells on e-bay for $180. Messick starts off the book by saying, **"The mob doesn't run this town. The mob owns it."**

Messick's findings heated reporters to a froth. They searched for supporting material and inflammatory stories. Hank Messick reported seeing Ben Novack attending a lunch or two with Lansky and created a back draft of epic proportions. Novack sued the *Miami Herald* with accusations of libel. The *Herald* put the lawsuit to rest with a front-page explanation of their opinion. The two short paragraphs explained their opinion was opinion and the lawsuit was closed.

Meyer Lansky chose the Imperial House as his residence for several reasons. The building has a similar curve and style to the Fontainebleau, as Melvin Grossman, a colleague of Morris Lapidus, built it in 1963. He lived on the second floor because it possessed three exits and no balconies that could be scaled in the middle of the night while he was sleeping. In addition, the lobby security was tight. The building is still famous on the beach, as it was never tampered with by any conversions or alterations, leaving it as it was built. The one-bedroom apartments are 1,500 square feet; the two bedrooms are over 2,000. Long after Lansky's death, Imperial House front doorman Daniel Hyde remembered the legacy left by Lansky. He heard many stories from long time resident Fay Stein who herself set a record with three other residents. Stein lived to 105, another resident to 104, and yet another is continuing strong as of this writing at 103; all three were neighbors in the Imperial House. Stein lived as a neighbor to Lansky and one time asked a favor of the former gangster. Stein was short on cash and asked Meyer to cash a check for her. He responded with a concern for his neighbor, not wanting to start any trouble for her. He simply gave her the cash and refused her check.

Meyer Lansky was known to leave the Imperial House every morning and walk his tiny dog, Bruiser, up and down Collins Avenue. He was purposefully trying to give the appearance of a normal, law-abiding life to the authorities. When he was younger, his day of business transactions was mostly carried out at his Fontainebleau poolside cabana, in addition to the card room inside the hotel. His home phones were known to be tapped by the FBI so he was known to use the Fontainebleau payphones for his mob business.

Mob boss Meyer Lansky's daily business operations spread the image that Miami was a city that didn't follow traditional organized crime territorial business rules. After Al Capone was sent to prison on charges of tax evasion, Lansky changed his methods of operations to evade the FBI. Soon thereafter he began his understated lifestyle where he laid low and lead a steady, traditionally humdrum lifestyle.

As it turns out, Meyer's widow, Teddy, was known in the Imperial House building to never open her mouth.

Ever.

That is, until Meyer died, then she was known to never shut it.

The view from Meyer Lansky's apartment was relaxing and easy.

At the age of eighty, he passed to lung cancer and was found to be worth close to nothing on paper. The FBI estimated his worth at $300 million.

It was common knowledge that **Frank Sinatra** was a regular performer at the Fontainebleau. It was common gossip that Sinatra was connected with the mob. Ben Novack was also part of that murmuring buzz. There were locally known, "Rumors that the Mafia controlled the Fontainebleau. Indeed, a 1961 report by the Florida Attorney General's office called the **Fontainebleau a 'hangout for hoodlums'**." (Cohen 2002)

The desire to make gambling legal at the Fontainebleau was not just popular with hotelier Ben Novack, it was popular with the second owner, Steven Muss. He was highly active in trying to get the dice on the books, as was evident with the Let's Help Florida Committee, that put the matter of **legalized gambling** up for vote in the November election of 1978. The committee ran a $2 million campaign saying that revenue from an increase in tourists would be $7 million higher if gambling were legalized.

As hard as the attempt has been to change the books, the hoteliers tried.

Mob activity at the Fontainebleau was not hung outside on an advertisement banner but the activity was known. Gambling was illegal in the state of Florida, but traditional, everyday business practices proved different inside the Fontainebleau's walls. Many hotels on Miami Beach at the time were commonly known as betting grounds.

The connections were deep at the Fontainebleau. In the retail stores, contacts were made. The lingerie and linen shop was run by a Max Raymond, a former inmate at Leavenworth Prison. His infamy came from connections to narcotics, burglary, gambling, and vehicular homicide. The stock exchange office was a rumored front and cover for unspoken activity. Published reports showed CIA agents met in a poolside cabana with Chicago mob man Giancana on the plan to assassinate Fidel Castro.

Swifty Morgan was always a call away if needed at the Fontainebleau. As the documented inspiration for writer Damon Runyon's character, The Lemon Drop Kid, Swifty was living out his retirement at the Fontainebleau pool. Runyon studied and wrote about gamblers, hustlers, gangsters, and actors. Swifty Morgan was a little bit of them all. Swifty could be seen daily walking around in his beloved Panama hat, trimmed grey goatee, walking cane, and dark mysterious sunglasses. Bluntly put, he was known as the local pawn man with high trade abilities. Card games at the Fontainebleau's card room and cabanas were known to make or break a man. Several hotels were known to change hands as the stakes of just another hand of cards. Swifty could cash in the previous night's card game, swapping out an original piece of fine jewelry or land parcel for cash. If you ask a local you could find any connections you needed at the Fontainebleau.

Ben Novack himself used his connections with clientele in his everyday life. It's been said that once he gave his **wife Bernice Novack** a beautiful gift as a reminder of his seldom seen soft side. Bernice was a former New York fashion model, stood tall and graceful, accenting Ben's arm with glamour and style. She was a breathtaking beauty, elegantly groomed with perfect features and proportions. Her appeal was elegance combined with beauty and youthful essence. Her features were a combination of Jacqueline Kennedy and Jennifer Love Hewitt with a stance that defined femininity. If you ask a local, it's commonly said that Novack married up.

Even today Bernice is known as a classic 1950s lady. She is talked about as a lady who is always impeccably dressed and beautiful. She doesn't, however, tell any tales of her days at the Fontainebleau. As the locals say, she'll take those to her grave.

Ben Novack summed up the asset of Swifty Morgan as the on site swap-man. With a gifted pair of diamond earrings Novack added the comment that Bernice could swap them with Swifty if she wasn't fond of the present. Novack was also documented as the husband who granted his wife gold plumbing fixtures for her birthday while she was out of the house for the day. On the other hand, Novack was regularly known to have high volume encounters throughout the day. Numerous things like shoes, a sofa, and even a grand piano were known to spontaneously fly out the window of his suite. The television that flew out the window was not from Novack, however. That was the action of Frank Sinatra over a room service tray. Sinatra was also known to throw the patio furniture off the balcony if it wasn't the style he liked.

Even after Ben Novack and Bernice divorced, his love for her was evident. His financial predicament was a well-known fact and his situation was bleak. In 1983 he liquidated his storage units located in Liberty City, where he held many Fontainebleau items. These items in holding sold at auction while the Fontainebleau hotel stood in distress crying from her leaking roof and showing her age spots as the paint peeled. The auction pulled a solid figure from the 500 attendees. Novack's goal from the sale was to buy something nice for Bernice, even though they were no longer together.

After bankruptcy, Novack sold the **Fontainebleau registered name** to buyer Stephen Muss for $1 million. With this he opened a new venture.

He opened a theme park in Boynton Beach with the theme and name of **Alcatraz**. Opened in a former A&P Grocery, Alcatraz was an entertainment jail. A warden welcomed the customers and immediately booked them as prisoners. Mug shots were taken and prisoners were led to their cell. Each cell was similar to a real prison were a toilet seat posed as an extra seat and a mesh screen separated any hanky panky. Prison guards served the food and after the meal, prisoners were led to the yard for entertainment, which was a life-sized game of billiards with a crocket mallet cue.

It wasn't long before Alcatraz of Boynton Beach was busted. Novack moved on to concessions at the public golf course in Hollywood, a city a few miles north of Miami Beach. The once famous king of the Fontainebleau, the man responsible for the grandest hotel in the nation, lived out his last days at a concession stand on the golf course.

Chapter 11
The Famous Fontainebleau Guests

The Fontainebleau has always been filled with famous people, right from day one. Popular groups like the **Rat Pack** of the '50s were **commonplace** at the hotel. Now individual celebrities travel to the hotel but don't come in teams of well-known faces, they instead travel in teams that include makeup artists, publicists, and bodyguards.

If you ask a local, Sammy Davis Jr. was the nicest and most down to earth of the bunch. He was relatable and didn't carry an aloof attitude or feelings of elitism.

Frank Sinatra was popular to say the least but he carried a side seldom seen but often feared. Sinatra was seen around the property with several well-dressed large men. The facts were simple, they were his employees and he was often involved in whispering comments connected to underground business dealings.

If you ask a local, the stories about Sinatra are abundant. One man gives Sinatra credit for saving his life. He saved his life when he told his employees to stop pounding on the man's face.

Stuart Blumberg tells a fascinating story about the night the local kid was pummeled. Sinatra had a close friend who was at one of the houseboats across the street from Eden Roc. Frank called the neighboring front desk kid working the midnight shift.

"Eden Roc."

"Ahhh… I need you to go across the street to the house boat and tell Jilly Sinatra wants him."

"Who am I talking to?" the desk boy responded.

"This is Frank Sinatra."

"Yeah, okay. Sir, I'm on a shift." The boy hung up the phone.

Not used to treatment like this, Sinatra immediately called back.

The phone rings.

"Eden Roc."

"Don't do that again." Pause. "This is Frank Sinatra and I want you to go across the street and get Jilly to come over here."

"Sir, I don't care who you are. I'm not leaving my shift. I have a job to do. Thank you very much." With that, again, the young boy hung up the phone.

About ten minutes later the Eden Roc front doors opened and two very large, very well dressed gentlemen walked with purpose through the doors and up to the front desk.

"You the kid that answered the phone before?"

"Yeah. Why?"

Without another word the poor young boy was pummeled to a bloody mess. It cost Frank Sinatra somewhere in the range of $10,000 to get the boy's jaw wired up and reset.

Each celebrity was another face and another encounter. Some old bellhops remember certain guests who didn't look like much but were flowing with ample tips. One particular story involves a bellhop, Levi Forte, and a guest who was looking quite shabby. The guest didn't appear to have any money as he arrived and then roamed the hotel looking tattered. One particular bellman took his bags and paid attention to the gentleman throughout his stay. When the man checked out, he left the bellman a tip of the highest standard. He bought him a Cadillac with the afterthought of, "I dress like this on purpose so that I don't attract attention. It also allows me to see who the true people are, not just those blubbering for a tip."

Dean Martin, who had a quick whit, could come up with humorous lines as readily as other people take a breath. When he was on stage with his buddies, the Rat Pack, he held stage presence. His tall stature and solid, muscular build made his stance strong and confident. He was known to pick up little Sammy Davis, Jr., cradle him in his arms like a baby doll, and say, **"I'd like to thank the NAACP**

for this wonderful award." That was traditional Dean Martin spontaneity and quick whit.

The Fontainebleau opened with a promise of shiny new excellence brimming with celebrities. Jimmy Durante, Jerry Lewis, and even Bob Hope lounged poolside drinking tropical elixirs equipped with mini umbrellas, all the while cracking jokes.

At the time, segregation was in full swing, yet Sammy Davis Jr., Louis Armstrong, Aretha Franklin, and Dianne Warwick were celebrated performers entertaining the guests. Once the show was over, they had to leave via the back door and head across the bridge to the Overtown area of Miami, then called Black Town. The real trick was still in the performers' pockets.

They were awake and buzzing from their show, not ready for a long restful night of sleep so they made their own jam sessions in Overtown. The real joke was the elite clientele at the Fontainebleau were seeing a high-class show at an equally high-class price but the better show was to be had in Overtown when self-conscious inhibitions were absent, attitudes were relaxed, and toes were tapping.

Jilly's houseboat was across the street from the Eden Roc. The houseboat in front of the Fontainebleau where they filmed *Surfside 6* was a massive two-story rectangle that looked like an oversized box of matches and nothing like a boat.

Encounters at the Fontainebleau can be seldom topped. Eighty-three-year-old Molly Weeks said, "When I was younger, my girlfriend and I went to the Fontainebleau one day to the bar. We looked up and Frank Sinatra was sitting right there next to us. She piped up right away and said, 'Frrrrrrrrrrrraaaaaaaaaaaaannnnnnnkieeeeeeeee, can I have your aaaaautooooooograaaaaaaaaaph?' He didn't like that of course, but he was nice and still gave it to her. He had all these beautiful women hanging onto him—of course! He was Frank Sinatra! I went over to him later and asked him, Mr. Sinatra, can I have your autograph? He liked that when you called him Mister."

When locals went to the grand hotel for a day of adventure, it was common to bump into a high rolling celebrity. That's part of what made the Fontainebleau so great. It was commonplace to hit on a girl at the pool only to later find she was the wife of … or the girlfriend of … the place was brimming with icons.

Ben Novack's second building held architectural presence.

The Rat Pack was made up of **Sammy Davis Jr., Peter Lanford, Dean Martin, Frank Sinatra,** and **Joey Bishop.** Together the young comedians were known as a social group in their early years of domination. They spent many days here in the Fontainebleau both on stage and as vacationing guests. When the calendar turned to 1960, the Rat Pack team was booked steady at The Sands Hotel in Las Vegas. The group performed as a team but also continued their own careers independently of each other. Their show was a chaotic mix of comedy and music. To the untrained eye they appeared to be drunk on stage but many members of the team made comments when they were well into retirement that it was part of the act. CNN reported Joey Bishop's, "Comedic schooling came from vaudeville, burlesque, and nightclubs." Part of his independent career branched out into the nighttime talk show scene where his sidekick was young Regis Philbin. Together the men put "The Joey Bishop Show" on

the air. Philbin said, "It was the thrill of my life to be chosen by Joey as the announcer for his talk show on ABC back in the '60s. I learned a lot about the business of making people laugh. He was a master comedian and a great teacher and I will never forget those days or him."

Bishop's nighttime talk show lasted two seasons. Johnny Carson dominated ratings but saw the talent of Bishop and used him as guest host in Carson's absence 205 times.

Academy Award winning actress and singer, **Judy Garland** was often a guest at the Fontainebleau. Her famous role as Dorothy in *The Wizard of Oz* was filmed seven years prior to the birth of her first child, daughter Liza Minnelli. Minnelli was born to Garland and her second of five husbands.

Betty Grable was often on the hotel grounds enjoying the sunshine and relaxed attitude. The famous singer, also known as an actress, was a breathtaking beauty at poolside. Hugh Hefner admitted Betty Grable was the inspiration for his magazine, *Playboy.* With the presence of Betty Grable was the presence of her husband, the famous big band orchestra leader **Harry James**. James, conducting a big band through a Swing Era repertoire, often provided the backdrop for Frank Sinatra. In 1954, Sinatra's career was catapulted forward with the presentation of an Academy Award for Best Supporting Actor. That same year, the Fontainebleau opened with the Grand Christmas Ball. Sinatra was a fixture from then on at the hotel. He was frequently linked to organized crime while his employees were often feared on sight for their swift, efficient, and quick beatings that produced the outcome desired for Sinatra. The New Jersey State Commission held a secret court session at midnight on February 17, 1970, where Frank Sinatra was questioned regarding organized crime. The outcome was not public knowledge.

Elvis Presley made a special appearance at the Fontainebleau. This was his first performance location after his service duty in the Army. He sang with Sinatra where they broke up the crowd by swapping each other's songs, Frank sang Elvis's famous "Love Me Tender," and Elvis sang Frank's famous "Witchcraft." The famous faces that filled the Fontainebleau seemed to be a steady stream of celebration. When Joan Crawford passed by, people were known to stand up and applaud. When the Beatles descended upon the property they carried with them a wake of giddy, screaming, swooning teenage girls. It was not uncommon to have President John F. Kennedy, President Lyndon Johnson, or former President Harry Truman on the property. If you ask a local, since the Fontainebleau opened, every president has been in attendance at the hotel.

The Beatles came to the Fontainebleau for a quick vacation in 1964 after their appearance on the "Ed Sullivan Show" filmed at the Deauville up the beach. The young longhaired rock group had a following of swooning teenage girls, screaming, crying, and hysterically shaking at the sight of the young men. The girls swarmed the hotel and were held back by security. It was no secret when the Beatles arrived, not even to Frank Sinatra as he was performing at the Fontainebleau's nightclub at the time.

Aretha Franklin loved to stay in Sinatra's suite as it had both a view and a great kitchen. Aretha loved to cook and was famous for bringing home cooked vittles to her rehearsals. She loved Miami because our international community gives shoppers the chance to buy any nontraditional ingredient right up the street. One day Franklin returned from her grocery run with a paper sack. As she was walking through the lobby the sack broke! Fresh pigs feet went sailing across the high glossed bow tie lobby floor. Aretha Franklin held her head high and just kept on walking.

Novack doubled his room occupancy with the addition of building two.

The Fontainebleau was like no other hotel in the world. This was the only place you could rub elbows with Elvis, Mia Farrow, and Presidents Nixon, Johnson, and Kennedy. To serve the famous clientele, there was a fine order to things including what food was served and where you slept.

It was no accident that Marilyn Monroe's suite was in room 1782 and John F. Kennedy's was suite 1784.

John Wayne was a hotel guest in 1964 when he was a selected guest speaker at the Republican National Convention. He returned here after his speech to sit at the Poodle Lounge. Joseph McGinnis, a reporter for the *Philadelphia Inquirer*, kept his recorder running at the bar. The Duke processed his speech and said, "What the hell did I say? I have no idea what the hell I said?" He pondered and gathered his thoughts from the speech, "Permissiveness is the biggest problem we have. The people in these colleges and these ghettos and these God dam longhair punks. Nothing is ever any different from how it ever was except all these punks get publicity." (*Time Magazine* 1968)

Pulling the celebrity faces to the forefront is not a difficult task at the Fontainebleau. The hotel doesn't kiss and tell, they hold privacy dear. Finding out who is staying there today is neither an easy task, nor a desired question. Privacy is key for the hotel as their obligation is to ensure a relaxing visit for all customers.

Regardless, pieces of history can be pieced together from locals visiting as well as preannounced intentions. Some celebrities like it to be known that they are there. **James Brown**, for example, was honored at the Fontainebleau in 2002 by the BMI Awards when they chose his musical impact as the reason for an ICON award.

The heavily accented décor on the south side of the Versailles building was a linear domination of rooms.

Historically, without needing to tally the votes, **Liberace** won the nonexistent award from the employees as the guest with the most and heaviest luggage.

The beloved **Ester Williams**, famous for her appearances in twenty-seven films was most popular for her synchronized swimming performances and swimming skills. Here at the Fontainebleau she performed poolside.

Joan Crawford was a well received guest who turned many eyes her direction. Her acting resume on the big screen won her many fans until her true story was revealed by her daughter in the book and movie, *Mommie Dearest.* Crawford was exposed as a neurotic, cruel, and overbearing mother whose tirades could be compared to demonic possession. While she was a guest at the Fontainebleau during her acting career she swooned around the hotel grounds carrying her makeup case. It wasn't odd for a high fashioned actress to carry a makeup case around but at the same time, it wasn't common for celebrities to employ a makeup artist and hair stylist. For Crawford, carrying her makeup case was a different version of cover up as was discovered by one of the bellhops. One day when she was floating through the hotel, the case popped open and little bottles of vodka fell all over the floor.

One of the most stunningly beautiful guests was **Elizabeth Taylor**. If you ask a local, one day she was walking down Lincoln Road with such breathtaking glamour that the patrons at the local cafes stood up and clapped as she passed. In 1963 Taylor became the highest paid movie star of all time with her $1 million role in *Cleopatra.*

Fontainebleau quickly became a household word. The **Miss Universe pageant** used the hotel as an on site location. Symposiums and conferences were a regular mainstay at the hotel, running the whole spectrum of topics from gathering morticians who filled the lobby with headstones to The Annual Mayors Conference. In 1958, John F. Kennedy attended the United States Conference of Mayors. Senator Kennedy spoke in the Fleur de Lys Room while Jacqueline Kennedy watched from her chair,

pregnant with their soon to be baby daughter they would name Caroline.

The Symphony Club began their tradition with the hotel right in their first year of business in 1954 with the Soiree Symphonique. The President of the Symphony Club Ball was Mrs. Mitchell Wolfson, a local resident from the prominent Wolfson family. The Wolfsons were business moguls with their prime business being Wometco, the owner of the prominent national movie theater chain and WTVJ television before it became NBC. Mrs. Wolfson's parties and balls were always grand affairs. The first Symphony Club Ball was attended by Queen Soroya, General James Van Fleet, the Shah of Iran and the Baron and Baroness Stackelberg.

The Chez Bon Bon Coffee Shop was a continual stopping spot for guests as a place to sit and chat.

Cabanas were rented by local families to stay at the beach for the summer school break. If you asked the employees of the hotel, they were often used for private extra curricular activities while businessmen were away from their wives.

Michael Aller remembered his youth in the Fontainebleau. The most peculiar thing he remembered was a group meeting for a function on roughly the fifth floor of the hotel. One of the VIP guests was gifted a motorcycle by an honoring organization that shall remain nameless. As most motorcycle gifts go, the recipient immediately jumped on board for a quick spin. He straddled the bike, started up the engine with a harmonious humm, lifted his feet of the ground, and took a quick tour where he hit a maid with the bike. It was just a swipe, she wasn't hurt, but she still needed to go fill out an accident report. When she went downstairs she said, "I just got hit by a motorcycle on the fifth floor." Of course the comment raised some eyebrows. They thought she was tilting the bottle on the job but she insisted she was sober and telling the truth. Hotel staff and security immediately went upstairs to inspect the scene of the hit and run accident and to see the motorcycle. They found nothing. Absolutely nothing. Everyone was gone.

The north side was loaded with spite. The aesthetic architectural design of The Spite Wall was visible from Collins Avenue.

Chapter 12
The Changing Faces of the 'Bleau

In true Fontainebleau style, the hotel grounds changed throughout the years as it morphed to meet the needs and desires of hotel owners and their guests. This is specifically evident in the **history of pools** at the Fontainebleau. In the beginning Ben Novack's plan was to entertain and awe. He built **two outdoor pools** sitting right on the ocean. Both were enormous in size and served a different purpose. The pool by the cabanas was dedicated to adults, diving off the high springboards, and strutting the latest swimsuit fashion as you descended the grand sweeping staircases from the second floor cabanas. The second outdoor pool was in the shape of a kitty cat. The cat took up the space by the ocean at the northeastern section of the property. The **kitty cat kiddy pool** didn't have nine lives; it had one short life that lasted less than four years. It was removed for Ben Novack's new building possessing The

Spite Wall. Women were known to swim, sleeking around their men in cat-like form while they purred and quietly meowed. Novack later added an indoor pool with 250 indoor sun lamps. When Steven Muss purchased the hotel out of bankruptcy, he changed the whole aura of the hotel. He added an enormous shamrock shaped pool the size of three tennis courts with a rock grotto incorporated theme. The **Lagoon Pool** was accented by in ground hot tubs with equally dominating rock accents.

The pool was well beyond normal pool size and standards. It housed a rock grotto with a second story waterfall bellowing over and into the pool with enormous strength. The same waterfalls existed in the hot tubs. The pool was at least three times the size of a normal competitive swimming pool. The billowing waterfalls created a playful atmosphere. An island with palm trees and tropical plants was

situated in the large pool but the best aspect of all was built a few years later as an additional water park.

Local historian and Historical Museum associate, Pepe Menendez said, "I approved the pool for the city. We had to give them variances because some of the stuff wasn't in the code. A lot we couldn't approve because it was against the health code. They wanted to do like in Mexico where the waiter would come serve you in the water but it wasn't approved." (Oral Interview, 11/13/06)

The pool island was originally planned as part of an in-pool dining experience.

Coconut Willies was a Mediterranean café that was always showcasing a live band. Music along the boardwalk attracted attention as well as covetous onlookers.

Opposite page:
The rock grotto was a wonderland of fantasy.

Stephen Muss introduced **Cookie's World** to the world. Cookie was a 7,000 square foot octopus built and designed for the children but enjoyed by everyone.

Muss gave the name Cookie to the octopus as it was the name used for his daughter Melanie as a child. Melanie worked for Stephen Muss at the time.

This deep sea creature was made the good old fashioned way – with concrete and paint. He hovered up above the kiddy pool at least seven feet in the air, floating as if he was performing a magic trick. The mere existence of the octopus invoked a festive atmosphere. His roughly twenty-foot girth was dwarfed by his enormous tentacles that waved out across the kiddy pool area. Underneath him was the flowing river intertwining in and out of grottos and foliage. As children and adults floated along, the octopus' tentacles sprayed down cooling water as you drifted underneath.

Cookie was an enjoyable shallow splash pool for toddlers while the intertwining rafting river that surrounded her had a perfect three foot depth.

Years later water spraying dolphins were added.

The octopus, much like the ice rink, was short-lived. During her brief life, Cookie was much adored and well used, but she was put to sleep when the hotel was bought by Turnberry Associates and six new pools were added to the grounds.

None of Cookie's great aspects equaled the **water slide**. The staircase was secretly hidden inside another faux rock formation stretching high above the octopus into the blue sky. The tropical plants growing in the rock face made the whole scene more realistic. After climbing the enormous stairwell, you stood high above the ground just below Heaven. You, and only you, stood right there next to God. You weren't standing on a balcony in a safe enclosed porch with a thirty-story building at your back. You stood in the open air. Air in front of you, air behind you, air to your right, and air to your left. It was almost like standing at the top of the ladder on the lookout tower with nothing to see but the soft smile of divinity shining down.

The view was not just the tunnel twisting down into nowhere, it was a vantage point. The rock at your feet bellowed the victorious climb of Mount Fontainebleau. In front of you were the treetops creating separation from the vast aquamarine glowing goddess. The white curling breakers in the Atlantic matched perfectly the white puffy clouds overhead. The blue sky and the aquamarine ocean stretched forever and beyond. The smell of the green treetops twirled a dance with the tropical flowers. The perfume was green and light. The soft breeze and the ocean spray energized every inch of exposed skin. This was no water slide; this was the most beautiful view of the ocean known to mankind. This pedestal, 260 feet high in the air, offered a moment.

This moment was personal.

One deep breath nourished any exhausted body. One deep breath equaled 30 minutes of yoga, four aromatherapy candles, dozens of fragrant roses, and 60 minutes of deep tissue massage followed by a relaxing sauna.

That's where you could stand and experience calm tranquility.

This is the same spot in the sky where a few feet away was the seething wall of concrete, sour with irritation and spite.

The 260-foot-tall waterslide was not to be confused with the rock grotto pool waterslide. The main pool's wa-terfall was originally built with much more entertainment than seen in the later years. When they constructed the grotto, they built a stairwell up the back, hidden in the rocks. At the top of the stairs was a cave to climb through and another water slide that wound down and twisted through the rocks. The passenger along for the ride shot out into the pool area like a bullet. The only problem was, the area where the slider entered the pool wasn't roped off and unknowing swimmers got hurt. They closed down that slide to prevent injury.

The grotto pool was first built in 1978; the slide was closed in 1981.

Underneath the rock grotto slide was another short lived, yet hidden treasure. In the mountain was a raw bar. You could swim in, have some food, and swim back out to the pool area.

Throughout the years, the pools weren't the only things to change. Each owner put his own taste into the hotel. When the hotel was built, it was one of a kind with no other competition in the world. With Steven Muss, the hotel was taken into a new dynasty of competitive vacation resorts. When the Turnberry team took the hotel they were working with a resort market that was cutthroat with intense competition. Through it all, the Fontainebleau has only gotten bigger and better.

The tubing was hidden amongst the faux rocks.

A small dumping pool was monitored by pool personnel in radio contact with pool personnel at the top of the slide.

The backside of the waterslide was a spacious grass lounging area.

When Stephen Muss bought the Fontainebleau, he renovated rooms, made the spa larger, and transformed the hotel into a market trendy condo hotel. A new tower was built, with condo prices starting at $300,000 and climbing to over a million dollars with a 40% presale rate that quickly rose during construction. This time on the beach was filled with escalating, jumping prices. Buyers would visit three properties in the South Beach area on the same day, only to find two were already sold. Properties were moving like a fresh batch of cookies. Decisions were made fast so as to not lose a property that could potentially work. Many people cashed out on their properties, doubling and even tripling their profits, depending on when they purchased. As sale prices climbed, property values soared, which increased property taxes. This created a problem as many property owners were overcome with tax expenses on their homes and were forced out in tears.

Following the boom was the inevitable bust. Property sales came to a screeching halt. All but the Fontainebleau's sales, they were going strong. As the real-estate market moved at a snail's pace in late 2006 and drudging through 2007, the Fontainebleau was untouchable. It appeared the property owners couldn't build their units fast enough. Properties were selling long before even the new ocean front tower was completed.

In the growth spurt of 2005, Miami Beach was experiencing the third property explosion in its lifetime. Beach properties were rehabbed and new condominiums were being built to cash in on the hot real estate boom. The city of Miami was filled with sky-high cranes. Driving through the city was like driving through a construction haven spanning miles upon miles. Cranes dominated the scene with a count of over one hundred in the simple drive up US-1. As quickly as the big trucks hit the scene on Miami Beach, the progress froze in time. Literally during the 2006-2007 timeframe, builders slowed their building pace to a mere snail's pace of activity while they waited for the market to recover from the real-estate recession. If the building was under construction, a construction loan saved the builder thousands of dollars. None of this affected the Fontainebleau where trucks were still flowing in and out daily. Construction at the Fontainebleau continued at a hearty clip while it literally stopped everywhere else, mid-project.

Stuart Blumberg, President and CEO of the Greater Miami and The Beaches Hotel Association has a handle on the hotel activity and how it affects the city. "We're the only city that I know of that has reinvented itself three times. Each recreation in its own period of time was a great success." (Oral Interview, 10/10/07) Blumberg has worked in the hotel market for just shy of fifty-two years. He started off his career as a summer bellman in 1956 when he applied for a position at the then new Americana Hotel (since, the Sheraton Bal Harbour), another Morris Lapidus hotel. When Blumberg began his job, he was planning on continuing his college education to someday become a lawyer. His career swerved into the hotel sector where he has made a dynamic impact, including his affect on the Loews Hotel.

Blumberg said, "The Fontainebleau was an unheard of hotel in this area. That's how I met my wife. She worked for Morris Lapidus." He was taken with the newest addition to the beachfront when the property opened. At the tender age of seventeen, he snuck into the grand opening and was awed with the glamour, the chandeliers, the grand lobby, and the glamorous guests. He did the same with the Eden Roc when it opened the following year and caught the show by opening performer Harry Belafonte. This was just the start of his sneaking in days. While in high school and with his local buddies they devised a working plan to meet girls at the Fontainebleau. "We got dressed up in suits and ties.

At the entrance of the pool you had to go through the stock market where the guys, the wise guys, would sit there all day in their bathing suits and watch the stocks with an attaché case. We looked good. The guard would say, 'where you going?' and I would say, 'to check my stocks'." Imagine that, a group of young high school seventeen-year-olds, dressing the part, breaking into the hotel to check their stocks, all as a front to pick up the hot chicks. "We'd run into the pool deck. Meet the young ladies who invited us, change in the cabana, and go swimming for the day. That was the place you had to be!" (Oral Interview, 10/4/07)

The chateau skeleton hasn't changed through the years, but the pool grounds have continually been improved.

Chapter 13
Filming

The movies that were filmed at the Fontainebleau were win, win situations. They advertised the Fontainebleau and they advertised Miami Beach. The hotel was such a glamorous location that producers would comment on the backdrop saying, "I don't have to change a thing to film here."

In **1960,** *The Bellboy* was filmed on site with Jerry Lewis playing a bellman named Stanley who joked and goofed his way through the day. He tripped over countless yapping dogs as the awkward and clumsy Stanley took them for a walk. Lewis starred in and directed the film. Ironically, the bellboy of the Fontainebleau, Floyd "Mac" McSwane, played the bellboy in the movie *The Bellboy*. Mac worked at the Fontainebleau throughout his life from the time when the Fontainebleau opened up into his mid-eighties during Stephen Muss' ownership. It was Mac who could agree with the longstanding Fontainebleau joke that the man who dropped his quarter on the lobby floor *denied it was his quarter* when the bellman picked it up and handed it back. It would cost him a dollar tip just to get his quarter back in his own pocket.

"Surfside 6" was filmed across the street in a houseboat parked in Indian Creek. One cast member played an additional role as an entertainer in the Boom Boom Room across the street. The famous detective series ran seventy-four episodes from 1960-1962. Lee Patterson, Troy Donohue, Van Williams, Diane McBain, and Margarita Sierra, the popular actors, were frequently seen around town.

In 1964 *Goldfinger*, starring Sean Connery, filmed in room 1114 and a famous pool scene where the glamorous hotel was displayed in all her glory from breathtaking helicopter views. The 007 film was famous for many top technological toys as well as the popular poolside poker game where women showed a controversial amount of skin.

In 1983 ***Scarface***, starring Al Pacino and Michelle Pfeifer, portrayed the famous gangster lifestyle on Miami Beach. In the film, Pacino sits down poolside at the Fontainebleau with the rock grotto waterfall in the background. This movie was filmed prior to the addition of the boardwalk separating the hotels from the beach. The film has grown in fame throughout the years and stands today as a documentary for the beach.

Throughout the years, *Scarface* has become more and more popular, breaking many rules of filming. The movie was directed by Oliver Stone at the same time he himself was struggling with his own addiction to cocaine. Al Pacino's character was fictional, depicting a Cuban Marielito Tony Montana. The criminal glamorized the cocaine trade while belting out an enormous number of foul words including using the F word a reported 207 times. For this reason, as well as the extreme violence, *Scarface* was originally tagged with an X-rating.

In 1992 ***The Bodyguard***, with Whitney Houston and Kevin Costner, was filmed on site in the La Ronde Room. Houston starred and sang, "I will always love you" in a tear provoking scene.

In 1994 ***The Specialist*** was filmed on site with Sharon Stone, Sylvester Stallone, and James Woods. Warner Home Video tagged the movie with, "The government taught him to kill. Now he's using his skills to help a woman seek revenge against the Miami underworld." This is the movie credited for the purchase of Sharon Stone's home on Star Island where she is a neighbor to Stallone.

The variety in architecture allowed variety for filming.

Morris Lapidus designed room for architectural aesthetics as well as enabling maximum views for visiting guests.

Chapter 14
Thinning Coin

Recounting Novack's downfall is often the game of mental tennis for locals. Some locals have solid opinions on Ben Novack. He was a strong businessman and as business goes, Novack was often over extended, particularly in the mid-1960s and '70s. Novack was trying to advance his fortune with the Fontainebleau Park project that covered 400 acres west of the airport. At the same time, hotel attendance was down citywide. Then there was the Sorrento and the repair thereof. Novack wanted to make this smaller Art Deco hotel part of The Fontainebleau. This was not any old Art Deco hotel; it was one he himself built, The Sorrento Hotel. As described earlier, Novack was a penny pincher and a heavy fisted screamer. This worked for him but it also caused him problems. This one particular problem affected the biggest failure of his life. Novack was financially stressed while absorbing the Sorrento project. At this very unfortunate time, catastrophe happened.

When the Sorrento was under construction, the foreman took down the supports holding together the weight-bearing columns. The support structures were not cured yet and the wall came crashing down to the ground. Some people said the foreman's action was another example of Ben Novack trying to save money in all the wrong places while others stated that Novack was the type of guy to associate with off kilter individuals who would do this sort of thing on their own accord.

If you ask a local, the foreman was commonly known as a drunk. In fact, it was said he was drunk at the time the supports were removed. The foreman was uninsured and had no money. Novack paid for the problem out of his own pocket.

The bottom line was the foreman made an unforgivable mistake. Since the foreman couldn't cover any costs, and didn't have insurance, Novack paid for the expense out of his own pocket, which added to his financial burdens. As bad as it had gotten for Novack, his hotel was still the best equipped with recreational facilities on the beach. Locals still code named the hotel the Shangri-la-by-the-Sea. A room was roughly $42 a night and the pool bar was open after 5 p.m. , an unknown sight on the beach at the time. (Donated clipping, "Tourist Forgotten at Beach Hotels")

This incident happened at a most inappropriate time for Ben Novack and is credited as the final blowout leading to Novack's downfall. The builder responsible for the most successful hotel of all time is also known as the builder responsible for the biggest failure of all time. Ben Novack began running the financial sprint of his life.

When Ben Novack went into his foreclosure proceedings he was not surprised to see the paperwork on his doorstep. *The Sun Reporter* wrote, "Creditors filed a foreclosure suit Friday… It was the third such suit filed against the hotel in less than a year."

The filing was made in January of 1977. The very same week Ben Novack had a bit of a high wire act to accomplish. As part of a ninety minute live television broadcast by CBS entitled, "Evil Knievel's Death Defiers" a one-inch thick steel cable was stretched from the Eden Roc to the Fontainebleau's Chateau building at the west end of the curve. *The Sun Reporter* ran a headline on the 28th of January that read, "Don't Look." The next day the front page read, "HE MADE IT!!!" Karl Wallenda, the seventy-two-year-old circus performer, walked the 720-foot distance in gusting winds that peaked at twenty miles per hour. Six giant searchlights lit his way as well as illuminated his associate, Dave Merrifield. As a trapeze performer, Merrifield hung from a helicopter while he performed and hovered over the two hotels.

At the time Novack's finances were struggling, the beach was in a downswing, but the ocean still provided the greatest luminous views in America.

In 1960, the Fontainebleau was pulling a gross profit of almost $15 million a year. (Donated press clipping) Even so, Ben Novack told the local paper that even these highly profitable numbers there was impending failure on the horizon as seen from the surrounding hotels taking a downswing in business. Fontainebleau business had dropped to 70% occupancy rates, creating a bleak outlook if this was a continuing downward trend. Still the numbers were commented on as "pretty good business," by the hotel spokesperson. Novack blamed the drain on the taxes. "We're the top resort hotel in the world," he said, "but if other hotels go under, we're bound to suffer. A cure is needed now before it's too late."

(Donated press clipping) At that time Fontainebleau rates fluctuated from $11.00 per room per person to $200.00 for a suite, depending on room size, season, and event. Novack's opinion and drive was specific, attract the people. To do this **Ben Novack made alterations and upgraded**.

Novack wanted to follow the attitude of the country as the popular cry became fitness for health's sake. "In 1968 he bought the Sorrento Hotel immediately to the south and remodeled it into a spa, raising the total number of rooms at his hotel to 1,300 and the length of his beachfront to 1,200 feet, which makes it the largest privately owned stretch of sand on Miami Beach." (Redford 1970,

242) He put the hotel on a $2 million transforming budget that resulted in a **private club and spa resort named Fontainebleau Resort and Club**. In the 1960s transforming an entire hotel, name and all, to accommodate health was highly questionable.

The biggest alteration was the addition of the "healthatorium" which was a health spa complete with an on staff physician. The new health spa was fashioned with a full gymnasium, treatment rooms, staff physician, and dieticians.

Controversy didn't only come in the form of the questionable health makeover, it came in the form of a burning question for guests. How do I file this in my taxes?

Really.

Six smaller hotels were already flowing with the spa concept and the success was gaining momentum. "The Internal Revenue Service has ruled a businesmen [sic] who rests and recuperates on his physician's order in a spa may deduct the expense from his income tax." (Schnier 1961) Novack was trying to breathe new life into his hotel with a new market trend.

"This won't work as a tax-dodge," was Novack's response to the local paper. The reporter commented, "Nevertheless, this is a hot legal potato which probably will soon end up before the U.S. Supreme Court. On July 19 the U.S. Court of Appeals for the Second Circuit, comprising New York, Connecticut, and Vermont, unanimously ruled that

Fabulous Miami Beach

The new spa "healthatorium" had an extended southern property line wall that was loaded with windows.

food and lodging are not deductible income tax items – even on bona fide trips under a doctors' orders for convalescence." (Miller 1961)

The matter was a serious dilemma. "Tax experts, however, argue that since the law does not specifically disallow living costs undertaken on medical advice, deductions should be permitted." (Miller 1961)

The underlying reasoning for the transformation was not just that of promoting health, far from it in fact. Ben Novack had been experiencing an enormous influx of Fontainebleau gawkers. Hotel traffic from sidewalk strollers was creating a problem for him. He was changing the hotel so that he could close off the property to non-guests. He moved the point of entry from the front lobby to the sidewalk where he added a gatehouse fully equipped with a guard, ensuring privacy for invited individuals and hotel guests. On an average day, Novack's hotel was filled with 2,000 guests, 2,000 cabana occupants and night clubbers, and an average of 2,000 gawkers. "[Ben Novack] Insisted he was much more interested in ridding the Fontainebleau of **lobby loafers** than promoting the spa." He said, "Some of the people come in here and use our stationary, they even try and pick up their mail here." (Miller 1961) Many guests came just to jot down a quick note on the stationary to send to their covetous friends back home. (Schnier 1961) These lobby loafers, a.k.a. lobby lizards, were detested by the owner, but for them, a note saying *the weather's great, wish you were here* had more impact when it was written on Fontainebleau paper.

Ben Novack was the kind of guy that you could rile up into a frenzy. If he had an ulterior motive or agenda, he could leak his thoughts like a gushing faucet. If you asked him the right question to spark his charge, he could readily spit his words back into your face. This was evident when he told the reporter the hotel was not turning into a private health spa. "I suppose if I dropped a goldfish in the garden pool we'd be an aquarium. The spa is like Burdine's adding a shoe department." (Miller 1961)

With the addition of the new healthatorium spa, Novack opened a new club. This exclusively private, member's only supper club was opened to a limited, elite clientele. **Club Gigi** quickly became the coveted place to have on the agenda.

As for the healthatorium, it was both loved and criticized. As simple and traditional as the healthful concept appears, it wasn't taken with full praise in town. Many nearby hoteliers were skeptical of the big move. Herb Robbins, the managing director of the Carillon Hotel, the now famous **Canyon Ranch Living Condo Hotel**, expressed the common sentiment. Robbins said, "I have the feeling that people who come to Miami Beach for a vacation may not go to a place where the connotation exists that the other people are there for health purposes. But I wish Novack success. It might bring in another new market of people to this area. (Donated press clipping) The Carillon Hotel closed down years later and made a total transformation itself. The property was swept up and redesigned with the sole purpose of healthful rejuvenation. Today, the property caters to the uber-wealthy who can afford to take a four-month vacation on site. Blood tests are taken, along with a total physical, for the purpose of improving one's numbers. Time is dedicated to relaxing, replenishing, and rejuvenating health. The location is dripping with amenities and luxury. The Canyon Ranch slogan is "Power of Possibility," but if you ask a local you'll find it described as the place where "the wealthy get healthy." Canyon Ranch was received with so much favor that they added an additional tower on their six-acre health complex. The former managing director of the 1960s didn't fully realize the change in the market, as Ben Novack observed.

Still the 1960 Fontainebleau transformation was edgy. Health and fitness was not widely popular and was certainly not something everyone practiced. The local paper said as such, "It marks an end of an era for the Fontainebleau, from a deluxe hotel unequalled anywhere, into a health spa. Hotel owners are watching to see what comes of the idea." (Donated press clipping)

Once the transformation was made, recreation hit you in the face before you even exited the lobby. An **ice skating rink** was added just off the lobby and beautifully depicted the diversity at the beach as it connected the lobby zone with the outside pool. Floor to ceiling windows covered the walls on both sides of the rink, allowing visitors passing through the hotel to watch people ice skate and peer straight through to see people on the beach. A beautiful glimpse of the rink is shown in the 1964 movie *Goldfinger*.

The Fontainebleau was the only place in the world where you could ice skate and freeze your "dupah" off and then walk out the door, dive in the

Atlantic Ocean, and work on your tan. Not only was the rink the only place to mix the two most diverse seasons of the year, it was the biggest ice skating rink in the South. The only problem was no one came to the ocean to go ice-skating. Needless to say, the rink was short lived and didn't even see her fifth birthday before she was transformed into more retail space. The divided space was too valuable as storefronts to lie in wait for the handful of athletes who desired to skate.

An indoor bowling alley with five lanes was created for entertainment. There was nothing of the sort in the area at the time. This was a groundbreaking advancement. The indoor pool was equipped with 250 heat lamps in case it rained. Novack added to the outdoor tennis courts that filled the grounds on the southeastern corner of the property. A driving range accented the six tennis courts for the golf enthusiasts, complete with golf pro. Sitting areas were clustered throughout the French gardens. Novack told the local paper, "The idea of a spa encompasses a room to sleep, three low calorie meals a day, diet, physical exams, therapy and gym." (Donated clipping)

Prior to the change in hotel grounds with the healthatorium, it was common practice to see people bringing a sack lunch to the Fontainebleau just to eat and be part of the scene. The act became a nuisance. Ben had certain desires for his hotel and it showed in the décor. He hated furniture in the front lobby and only wanted the space to be used as a meandering flow-through. Sidewalk strollers would enter the Fontainebleau in the 1950s and early '60s to see what was happening at the La Ronde Room. This very act became such a huge annoyance to Ben Novack that he closed off his hotel and changed the whole attitude of the Fontainebleau. The area that is now a walk through serpentine hallway connecting to the Sorrento was closed off and fenced in, complete with a guard at a gatehouse. The front of the property was enclosed with a hedge or fence to keep strollers outside. Novack wanted spenders, not wandering gawkers, in his hotel.

Chapter 15
Financial Trouble For Ben Novack

Twenty years after Ben Novack built the hotel, he was **relieved from his position** at the Fontainebleau so assets could be liquidated and debts settled. At the time, the hotel was $29 million in debt in both secured and unsecured loans, $4 million of which was reportedly owed to the third mortgage holder, Roland International Corp. Novack was highly over-extended on the Fontainebleau. The hotel had a reported mortgage payment of $5 million a month. With this number in mind, remember that the Fontainebleau started out as a $20 million asset, owned by the bank. Fontainebleau's success brought the mortgage amount down to $7 million. Ben Novack turned around a few years later to leverage the hotel so severely that he was swimming in dangerous waters. He was stretched too thin, standard business challenges turned into huge financial issues, and the bankruptcy black hole swallowed Novack for lunch.

For seven months prior to the final workout date, November 22, 1977, Ben Novack was working with the courts to try and resolve his financial troubles. His efforts proved unfruitful. The U. S. Bankruptcy Court originally scheduled the final hearing for November 16, 1977. This meeting included two interested purchasing parties looking to rescue the hotel. Redevelopment Agency Vice Chairman Stephen Muss was working together with Roland International Corp. as one possible purchasing party. Roland International, the third mortgage holder, was the initiator of hotel receivership as their payments were severely behind. Oppenheimer Properties Inc., in New York, was the second potential purchaser, working with local banker and lawyer Shepard Broad. U.S. Bankruptcy Judge Thomas Britton oversaw the process. Receivership took affect seven months prior to the bankruptcy court date when Ben Novack was removed from control of the hotel and ordered to liquidate his assets to resolve his debts. Novack worked diligently with his lawyer, Irving Wolf, to resolve the matter.

A possible purchase of the Fontainebleau was a normal business venture for **Stephen Muss** as he was a prominent developer in the Miami Beach area.

Structurally the building stood solid.

He was known, he was good at what he did, and he knew how to get a job done. Muss has already changed the beachfront all along Collins Avenue, specifically in the Millionaire's Row section of town with the construction of the Sea Coast Towers buildings and The Alexander. He often worked as a team with his father, Alexander Muss. Together they built Towers of Key Biscayne and Towers of Quayside. All of these buildings were put up in a short span of years prior to the Fontainebleau project. Stephen Muss had just come to Miami Beach in 1963 to work with his father.

This time of potential purchase on the Fontainebleau was no small project for Muss considering his interests. During the late '70s Muss was a key player in the South Beach Redevelopment project, a dynamic plan to transform South Beach, specifically the area south of 5th Street, into a luxury resort. This project was commonly known as **The South of 5th Project** and was estimated to involve over half a billion dollars. The resort would literally change the dilapidated buildings known locally as the slums into an all-encompassing, entertainment extravaganza. Enormous, lavish buildings were planned with a new convention center, elaborate shopping venues, high end restaurants, and recreation sites including tennis courts. An intricate canal system was to wind in and out of the buildings complete with gondola taxis, fountains, and entertainment.

The *Sun Reporter* headline said a mouthful with the title, "The whole plan is to make South Beach a dream come true."

Total occupancy rates were not as high as previous years. This added to Novack's financial stress.

The image of paradise was glorious. "Imagine an area with the arty flavor of Coconut Grove, the fascination of the Monmartre section of Paris, the mellow beauty of San Francisco and her Fisherman's Wharf, the casual lifestyle of the Riviera, the unique waterways of Venice, and the class of Palm Beach." (Fleischman 1977)

As most things go, it wasn't all sunshine and roses. The project was under fire from many angles. The most vocal of the groups involved were the elderly residents living in the immediate area. One resident wrote to *The Miami Beach Daily Sun Reporter* on November 19, 1977, the very same day they ran the Fontainebleau's court date. The irate resident, Barney Rudnick, accused the agency of using, "unethical tactics, dishonesty, and deception." This was all focused around the concept that the re-development was not *re*developing but instead was kicking 6,000 elderly residents out on the curb, all for greed and in the name of making more coin.

Immediately following the pummeling tirade from the elderly resident was another article from Bernard Eilen, the President of the Hotel New Yorker. The response was blunt and to the point, presenting the critics as passionate lovers of slums and stagnation, using immature logic, narrow minded stupidity, and plain ignorance.

Between the three main issues at hand, the bankruptcy and purchase of the Fontainebleau, the complaints against The South of 5th Project, and the responses to progress, one thing held no argument. This one day of newspaper production was the type of day that was an editor's dream come true.

In the end, The South of 5th Project was punted for lack of funding and objections against the slums of Miami Beach. Negative criticism and lack of support came specifically from Janet Reno, State Attorney at the time. The bottom line was Reno didn't consider the area blighted. Meanwhile, Miami and Miami Beach were well known throughout the nation. Unfortunately we weren't known for the luxury hotels and beautiful ocean; instead we were known as the best place to buy cocaine, as well as the most likely place to be killed. Today the National Geographic Channel runs a historical documentary on the two-a-day murder tally resulting from the high flow of **cocaine** from Columbia. Not only was the murder rate causing us to break records, the price of cocaine itself broke records. So much cocaine was flowing through the Miami area that the price fell. The supply and demand curve was saturated with white powder. Three years later, over 150,000 Cubans flooded the beaches and port of Miami when Fidel Castro opened his prisons to release his undesirables through the Port of Mariel.

This time of redevelopment was vital to Miami Beach. The importance of Stephen Muss and his input in town was dynamic and monumental. To say Muss saved Miami Beach is an understatement. If he had been allowed to follow through with The South of 5th Project *and* the Fontainebleau, there's no telling where Miami Beach would be today. One thing is not up for debate; Stephen Muss changed the face of the beach.

At this sensitive time of bankruptcy, the two Fontainebleau purchasing interests stalled out the court date. In addition to these interested buyers, **Ben Novack and his lawyer Irving Wolf were pleading with U.S. Bankruptcy Court Judge Thomas Britton** to give them more time to **find investors**. Novack wanted to buy his own hotel back from distress. Ben Novack said, "We had many deals ready. But the press has killed it every time." (Dozier 1977) The court date was rescheduled and reconvened seven days later on November 22, 1977.

The hearing took all day.

Ben Novack and his legal team fought to the death trying to secure investors to save his hotel. His efforts proved to be valiant, but without success.

Hotelrama, Inc., a corporation made up of three business minds, was a solid player in the court ordered sale. New York real estate tycoon Harry Helmsley, local developer Stephen Muss, himself holding a 25% interest, and Roland International Corp., and their attorney Aaron Podhurst, offered the court $4 million in cash to, "assume responsibility for the remaining obligations to the point that the unsecured creditors, holding approximately $6 million in claims could receive about 61 cents on their dollar within 30 days." (Dozier 1977)

The Oppenheimer camp made their offer higher at $8.4 million cash but the closing date wouldn't be until April 30th.

The Roland team responded by saying they couldn't guarantee their offer would remain for ten days. A **third interested party** didn't receive much press at all. That party was a solid player and was headed up by Ben Novack himself. Novack had several investors committed to the project. Testimony was given showing the investors included three major participants. The first was a local, Ed Kogan, who was going to put in $1 million. Next, a physician from Venezuela was putting in $2 million. Lastly, a team of investors out of Columbus, Ohio, was made up of Amway Distributors and headed up by Abraham Claxton, who committed $500,000 from the independent Amway distributorship of Abraham Claxton and Associates.

For the record, it must be told that Ben Novack's son, Benny Jr., was a prominent businessman in the Amway world. As far as local opinion goes, some people thought he was different from most folks, some people had little to say, some people said he ran the Amway conventions and that was all, and some people say he's one of the wealthiest Amway guys ever known. Amway has overall sparked many strong emotions about their business, yet they have offered a business plan to millions of potential distributors, hundreds of thousands of which became enormously successful. Abraham Claxton was considered part of that crowd.

Judge Britton ordered a reconvening court date of December 2nd with all offers presented in writing and sealed to the court by 5 p.m. on November 29th. The judge stressed the final court date as December 2nd. He did *not* want this matter rescheduled, revisited, or argued any further; December 2nd was the final date for the Fontainebleau.

Ironically, on that same day of November 22, 1977, as the bankruptcy hearing was taking place, **The Fontainebleau grounds were under attack** by Wonder Woman and Super Man.

Literally.

The 22nd annual masquerade gala benefiting the Deed's Children's Cancer Clinic was whooping up their celebration with comic book characters in the famous Fontainebleau ballroom. The Flintstones were there, as well as, Batman, Star Wars Storm Troopers, and even Mickey Mouse was in town with his girlfriend Minnie. The characters were adults who designed costumes based on comic book heroes. Daddy Warbucks turned out to really be Bob Weaver, the local weatherman for Channel 4. As a matter of fact, 710 people were celebrating with laugher and jokes. Cartoons were projected on the wall while a juggler, a balloon man, and a clown entertained. All this was underway for the purpose of kicking up money to cure cancer. This joyful and purpose driven event was underway while the hotel they were in was on the chopping block.

In fact, the recent bookings at the Fontainebleau were enormously successful. Some opinions easily led visitors to believe the hotel was falling apart and in a horrific state of dilapidation. This was not true. It needed repair and was leaking in a great number of places, but the structure was sound and the facility was functioning.

The month prior to the final bankruptcy date proved successful for the Fontainebleau as they were fully operational as a hotel for the conventions. **During this time five major conventions used the Fontainebleau as their headquarters.** Each group needed to reserve a room block of 1,100 to be considered to use the hotel as headquarters; one group had 21,000 delegates. Praise and appreciation was reported back to the hotel by all five groups: The National Association of Theatre Owners, The National Association of Independent Insurers, The American Dental Association, The National Association of Realtors, and The Universal Federation of Travel Agency's Association. None of this, however, was front-page news. The front page was reserved for the horrific bankruptcy news. This news of success and steady, productive business was located in the Business Section of the *Daily Sun Reporter,* page 10.

All the official offers were made to the court in writing and sealed as the judge requested. The bidding deadline was held firm with the established November 29th, 5 p.m. deadline. The bids were recorded and thusly reported on November 30th in the *Daily Sun Reporter*. Oddly enough, the third bidding party including Ben Novack was a strong contender. Amway Distributor Abraham Claxton's sealed written offer totaled $28.8 million with a closing date of March 5, 1978. Ironically, Claxton was part of the same group that originally attempted to buy the Fontainebleau when the hotel first entered bankruptcy in April of the same year. This bid edged out the Oppenheimer bid of $26.3 million. The Hotelrama bid was not officially listed in the local paper but was referred to as a similar figure to the original offer during previous court testimony. One major difference in the Hotelrama sealed bid was Stephen Muss had bought out Harry Helmsley's share. This gave Muss a 75% ownership and Roland a 25% ownership.

Harry Helmsley and his notorious wife, Leona Helmsley, a.k.a. The Queen of Mean, were later indicted by U.S. Attorney Rudy Giuliani for tax evasion and extortion. Giuliani proved the couple upgraded their personal weekend getaway home at a cost of $8 million and billed the invoices to their hotel business as company expenses. Harry was deemed too ill and frail to stand trial. When he died he left his $5.5 billion empire solely to his wife Leona. Leona served her prison term and house arrest term before she died.

The Fontainebleau didn't rest, bankruptcy court or not, they still made the paper almost every day. Even though December 1st was a day of rest in Fontainebleau liquidation land, the front page was still occupied by an enormous Fontainebleau event. Literally. Several Circus Vargas elephants took a break from their Miami Stadium performance to swim in the ocean and then lunch at the Fontainebleau. The front-page headline for the *Daily Sun Reporter* on December 1st read, "Not your typical tourists…" The picture of the elegantly draped, linen clad table was filled with beautiful dishes of decadent food and lined up with trunk and tusk toting mammoth beasts along the side. Fontainebleau vice-president of marketing, Harold Gardner, plugged the hotel waiting for the bankruptcy courts decision when he said, "There are no problems too big for the Fontainebleau. We can cater to everyone."

Even on the announcement day, the Fontainebleau was booked to the brim with conventioneers as the Alternate Sources of Energy headquartered at the hotel.

The view has always remained.

Chapter 16

Stephen Muss

Many locals paid their traditional 15 cents for the daily paper with eager eyeballs the next day on December 2nd. Anticipation was high for the local boy, Stephen Muss. He was forty-nine years old and a capable, admired developer in the area, as well as a prominent political player. On his resume, Muss holds the position as chairman of the Dade County Sports Authority but his influence ran far deeper. In fact, Muss's political powers were so great, he was credited as the reason four City Commissioners for Miami Beach occupied their seats. Muss was a man known as a power player. His whole life was development and development on Miami Beach was Muss.

When Stephen Muss was a young eighteen-year-old, he left high school in New York to go work with his father. At that tender age, he started his position by breaking up bricks with a sledgehammer on the jobsite. Three years later, he was serving as president of the company. At the young age of twenty-one, he oversaw the construction of 10,000 homes and several shopping centers.

The court scene was diplomatic and productive. Stephen Muss had the selected bid. He purchased the hotel out of bankruptcy and promptly went to work. The Fontainebleau purchase labeled Muss as the largest owner of property on Miami Beach. Muss is a tall man with broad shoulders and carried an appropriate bark to achieve business intentions. He is the original definition of a formidable man. To say he often got what he wanted would be an understatement to his abilities. He was a serious, brilliant, business-minded man who worked hard to achieve success. He was not afraid to get his hands dirty and was often seen on the grounds getting down and dirty to meet hotel obligations.

The cost to purchase the hotel was $28 million, giving each room a price of $23,333. The hotel leaked in multiple areas for a variety of reasons, but the property and its history were dynamic. Stephen Muss considered the Fontainebleau Miami Beach's best asset and he proved his convictions. From the beginning, he understood the importance of having knowledgeable persons running the hotel operations. First he hired **Helmsley-Spears to manage** the property. Helmsley-Spears is a real estate company founded in 1866 that deals with multiple angles of real estate including hotel management. The company was operated, at the time, by Harry Helmsley, the same Harry Helmsley that Muss just bought out in the bankruptcy recovery offer. In 1978, Stephen Muss switched the management to **Hilton Hotels**.

Muss began throwing money at the hotel to bring it up to his standard of class. With $400 million he added everything imaginable to revitalize the hotel. As a third generation developer he was well trained and able to handle the enormous project.

When he purchased the Fontainebleau, it had fallen from grace as the grandest hotel in America. It was functioning as a capable and highly hospitable hotel that fully served conventioneers, but it was no longer sought out as a celebrity hangout in any sense. It was no longer the hot place to film a movie and most importantly it was no longer in top shape. It needed attention. One major project Hilton encouraged Muss to activate was to purchase the Eden Roc and connect the two properties via bridge, amongst other upgrades.

Prior to purchasing the Fontainebleau, Stephen Muss learned this aspect with extreme clarity. In the *Saving South Beach* book, M. Barron Stofik wrote about Muss' hotel stay at the Fontainebleau. He encountered a private visit in his hotel room that was *most* distasteful and *highly* uninviting. When Muss was in his room, his bathroom ceiling caved in on him. To make matters worse, a plumber fell through the ceiling immediately thereafter. He knew going into the purchase of the Fontainebleau that it was a project of love and dedication.

Meanwhile, back at the courthouse, Ben Novack was running around with flailing arms. "Appeal!" "Appeal!" He was begging for Bankruptcy Judge Britton for a stay on his decision.

Walt Dozier, the local reporter covering the Fontainebleau saga said, "Novack's appeal essentially claims that he was not given enough opportunity to participate in clearing the debt."

Larry Schantz, the attorney for Larry Gilbert, said if Novack was granted a stay they would request a bond of over $12 million. The opinion was pretty consistent between the legal contenders. The collective voice said, "You've had your day in court for over seven months now. Put the baby to bed."

Judge Thomas Britton denied to stay the sale unless Ben Novack came up with a $10 million bond by the coming Wednesday at 5 p.m.

Novack couldn't financially follow through and Muss took official ownership.

After the Muss team established hotel management with the Hiltons, once that hotel management was in place, the new management plan was launched. The Fontainebleau Hilton Resort charged $269.00 a night, $179 for off-season rates. In 1977, rental ads ran in the beach paper's classifieds ranging from $100 to $200 a month, $1,500 for the winter season October to May. It was popular for elderly residents to come to Florida and spend a two to eight month clip in the warm weather of Miami Beach. This snow birding season was a popular venue.

Reports on tourism were optimistic, but numbers for tourists "on the ground" were weak. "For the first seven months of this year hotel and motel occupancy in Miami Beach was down 3.2 per cent over last year." (Buckner 1977) Statistics reported a decline in tourism of 12% for the month of July alone. State numbers were up 6.1 %. The day following Buckner's article another report came from Tallahassee, the state's capital, stating a banner year for 1977 with predictions of a whopping 34.3 million Florida visitor for the following season. At the time, the nation as a whole was pulling out of the 1973-75 recession. Household income was rebounding with extra spending money. Employment numbers were strong and security sat on the horizon. **Vacations were becoming popular again**.

Stephen Muss immediately started repairing the hotel.

Miami Beach was actively attempting to cash in on the tourism ticket. Polls were taken attempting to establish creative measures to bring tourists to the beach. In the *Sun Reporter,* Julius Frishwasser reported six ideas rising to the top: 1) create an official city representative acting as a roaming concierge for elite visitors, 2) welcome gifts in hotel room, 3) hotel security, 4) promote television show site productions, 5) increase courtesy, and 6) create a police presence. Of course, these are all superseded by the most important proposal of all, honest legislators **coupled with legalized gambling**.

The main problem with cashing in on the tourism ticket was you needed a place where the tourists wanted to visit. Miami Beach was a risky gamble. Stephen Muss didn't scoop up the Fontainebleau for a song, patch some holes, and throw on some paint. He bought the hotel in a town that was a risky gamble, but had a beautiful view.

The Fontainebleau foreclosure year showed some pretty high crime in Miami Beach. A "ghost ship" was seized with thirty tons, $18 million worth, of marijuana on board. The Army Corp of Engineers was aggressively studying a project of sand replacement on the drastically eroded beaches. The project eventually took $110 million. Hotel hospitality employees throughout Miami Beach were revving up their second round of highly publicized strikes. Then, to make matters worse, the city counsel was presented with the issue of aggravated topless bathing … again.

The rock grotto shortly after construction. *Photo courtesy of Sidney Mehr.*

Muss added the rock grotto pool with waterfalls shortly before Cookies World.

City Councilman Phil Sahl, a man who was clearly an aged senior citizen, was quoted in the *Sun Reporter* at the council meeting. Sahl said, "In all candor, it caused me a lot of laughter at first. But after discussing it with several people, I said to myself, 'God's masterpiece is a well-built woman,' and Mr. Mayor if you look into it, you will see what I mean."

Today, Miami Beach knows Stephen Muss as a great developer and an even greater hotelier.

After Muss purchased the Fontainebleau, he wasn't received well by the press. He was a bold man who could be forthright, using aggressive words matching a gruff demeanor. This, of course, rubbed journalists the wrong way. *Tropic Magazine* dedicated their front cover to Stephen Muss with a full, dominating photo topped with the title "I'm Steve Muss and You're Not." The internal section dedicated to Muss focused on one primary topic, "the egomaniac" that owned the Fontainebleau.

This sort of journalism was highly effective in pushing back the enormous efforts of the Fontainebleau. The hotel was aged and hurting. Muss threw money at her to improve her image and grounds. Unfortunately, the news report from Miami were often horrifying, featuring incidents of violent crime at the hotel or in the city, stories of the cocaine cowboys, the marielitos, of tourist killings, or of the abuse of the elderly on the beach. These reports would go national and business was affected.

Lisa Cole said, "Miami Beach was on its knees. The Fontainebleau was the grand dame that needed a little botox. We would grow, build up the city, and then the media would report and we were back on our knees."

Muss remembered the glory days of the Fontainebleau from his father's stories. He knew he had the greatest hotel of all time on his hands and he wanted to bring her back to her glory days. He worked tirelessly to draw tourists back to Miami Beach. He sold conventions when there wasn't even a restaurant in town to send them to eat. He built up his hotel and put in his own restaurants. Guests would come and ask about dinner restaurants in town and the answers were thin. Two places existed outside the Fontainebleau's walls, Joes's Stone Crab and The Forge. As shallow as it looked, hotel employees recommended that guests stayed there to eat. But the truth was, they weren't going to get robbed and the food was good.

What is a seldom known and purposefully hidden character trait of Stephen Muss is that he is a man who understands how to create a functioning relationship with the City of Miami Beach. The city is very well known as being hard to work with and often

easy to irritate. Stephen Muss is the man responsible for changing city ordinances to allow outdoor dining, as we know it today. This activity was banned prior to Muss. This is a description of character as Muss didn't own any restaurants that had the potential to provide café seating on a sidewalk, but he did this work for the improvement of the city.

With the convention business that the Fontainebleau was aggressively cultivating, the City of Miami Beach hired a gentleman to expand and improve the Miami Beach Convention Center. He had Stephen Muss in his pocket as a free confidant, voice, and aggressive business tornado. Muss plugged the facility, worked the project, and succeeded in filling the place with functions. Together the two men doubled the size of the facility. Stephen Muss didn't make a dime off the center directly, but worked like a dog on the project because he needed it for his hotel guests.

Muss was such a prominent aspect of the center's success, the city dedicated the Miami Beach Convention Center to Stephen Muss. Huge letters stood out front and declared *Stephen Muss Convention Center*. They even put his name on the back of the chairs inside the facility. The city and Stephen Muss, however, continued to buck each other. Muss wanted the center to be run by private money; the city wanted the center to remain under their wings. The city turned on Muss, took his name off the facility, and the great, invisible, and unspoken-of divide that separated the two influential forces of Miami Beach was set in stone. Stephen Muss stood on one side, the city on the other.

This one act of name removal was one of the most aggressively rude acts of conduct to take place in Miami Beach. Purely political, this one thing affected countless others. To have a whole convention center dedicated in your honor and then to have it removed was a terrible blow to Stephen Muss.

While this whole ordeal was unfolding, Muss was active bringing business to the area by creating the Greater Miami Convention and Visitors Bureau. He is the one man given credit for creating a 3% tax on visitors that was used to market tourism in the county. His philosophy of putting money back into business until the business was running smoothly was reflected in this one act. The bureau is largely responsible for the success of the beach today. The Miami Beach Convention Center quadrupled in size as a result of the visitor's tax. In addition, the tennis area of Key Biscayne came to life and Coconut Grove's Convention Center was expanded. All of these developments affect the county in increased publicity and tourists. The effect was a snowballing success.

DADE COUNTY

BEFORE

AFTER

Beach erosion was a highly problematic issue that cost a handsome $110 million.

Once Stephen Muss took on the Fontainebleau project, he continued the family tradition. His daughter **Melanie Muss** left a highly coveted position with Estee Lauder to work with her father at the Fontainebleau and became the Vice President of Development for the Fontainebleau. She reportedly became the key component connecting Stephen Muss to Hilton Hotels and Turnberry Associates.

As far as business as usual was concerned, hotel guests enjoyed the newly popular entertainment sweeping the country called **dinner theater**. The neighboring Eden Roc was presenting "Musicana," a performance of singing and dancing for a ticket of $14 per person with accompanying drinks costing $1.75. The Fontainebleau had their own dinner theater in the La Ronde Superstar Theater with a staged performance by the famous actress **Barbara Eden**, known popularly from her hit television show "I Dream of Jeannie." Eden performed with comedian **Pat Henry,** pulling a ticket price of $12 per person, $30 for the New Year's Eve performance. Club Gigi showcased **Pia Zadora** at the same time with a ticket of $50 per person.

Chapter 17
The Muss Family Moves In

Stephen Muss and his family moved into the penthouse and took up residence in roughly half the top floor of the hotel. This wasn't an overnight move as Stephen Muss' personal life was in transition. When he bought the hotel he was on wife number two, a much-loved woman who was adored by the hotel staff and her own family. After her death, wife number three succeeded her, and then wife number four.

When the family moved in (wife number 3), they took over the Sinatra suite and added more connecting rooms to make a home. After some time, they added the floor below with a connecting spiral staircase. In the end, the Muss' took up the Chateau rooms 1500-1506 with the added few rooms on the 14th floor. The home eventually had multiple bedrooms, a personal gym, servants' quarters, and a working waiter's room. After the Turnberry purchase, the Muss' bought one of Lenny Kravitz's homes a few blocks up the island. The 15,000-square-foot house boasted a master bedroom with 1,800 square feet. He paid $14.5 million and threw in double that to make the home his own.

If you ask a local, after Muss purchased the Fontainebleau, the general day to day function of the hotel was the same. This included some of the stool renters at The Poodle Lounge. This time, however, the Madame of the Fontainebleau was known as a lady in residence. She relocated as the hotel closed down for total renovation in 2005. This was no monumental ground breaking news; it was standard life. Even in her advancement in years, she took pride in her appearance wearing black fish net hose, high, high heels, and animal print clothes that made her seductive features prowl. Everyone knew of her and loved having her around for multiple reasons.

One longtime local remembered working in the hotel gift shop downstairs as a young eighteen-year-old. One day on the job, a huge man well over six feet tall walked through the shop door. It was not likely, but possible for unfavorables to find their way onto the grounds, including street vagrants.

Employees had been instructed on how to deal with situations that arose from time to time and the staff member hoped to do the job well. The man in the gift shop was a bit of a towering beast and looked quite unsightly. His white hair was frazzled and unkempt. His clothes were dirty and tattered. His shoes were an unspeakable mess, falling apart, and filthy. To add kerosene to the fire, the man carried a nose retracting, milk-curdling stench. The Fontainebleau was an establishment of superior quality and service. This was no place for vagrants to come in from the heat. Security was immediately called to have the man gracefully removed. When security arrived, their eyes popped at the sight of the man.

It was Stephen Muss, owner of the Fontainebleau, a man who was comfortable getting his hands dirty to take care of his hotel.

Muss was a hands on owner in every sense of the word. He contributed a $64 million renovation to the hotel area and grounds. This infusion changed the hotel and brought life to the grounds. The heavy curtains were removed from the enormous windows to showcase the hotel's best asset, the ocean. With this first move in the Muss chess game, the hotel took on a breath of fresh air. The lobby instantly transformed into a shinier, happier version of itself.

Families were traveling more in the late 1970s and early '80s. Children running around the hotel grounds was a normal sight. Muss saw a need and filled it. He added a whole new playground of sorts. A waterslide was added but hidden in a rock grotto structure so that it blended. The staircase was encased in faux rock and the tubing was accented with more faux rocks to complete the already established rock grotto theme. **Cookie's World** was completed for the children as a colossal octopus that rose up over a meandering river perfectly formed for an easy floating tube adventure. The river wound around tropical foliage and under octopus arms. Refreshing spray came down from the tentacles as a cooling flow of water doused the children. Most parents wouldn't dream of letting their children float alone, not when they could jump aboard themselves on adult size rafts. The famous Fontainebleau turned into the long lost recess for vacationing adults.

One thing was specifically particular to the Fontainebleau with the addition of Stephen Muss. The kindness in hotel staff and courtesy to others was highly prominent. Miami and Miami Beach has often been accused of being a bit of a rude city. The reason has often been attributed to the enormous flow of visitors, with numbers reaching into the millions on any active weekend. When millions of people upon million of people wildly trash your city week after week, you tend to get tired of treating them kindly. After a drunken tourist or two keys your car, as a local, you tend not to smile at everyone who passes you in the street. The cause for rudeness has also been blamed on the fact that most folks don't speak English. Day after day, this tends to be frustrating and you begin to take care of yourself without looking out for others. The Fontainebleau, however, rose up against the rude. The staff has consistently been exceedingly helpful and beyond friendly. This civility is a breath of fresh air, wafting a contagious happiness that is an inspirational feeling for the city.

One of the most loved occasions for the hotel was the marriage of Stephen Muss' daughter, Heather. The wedding housed 1,200 guests at the hotel and started off with a 6,000-square-foot raw bar with accompanying drinks. Guests mingled and drank for a couple of hours before the wedding. Decorative two-foot long fish sat amongst mounds of shrimp, each three inches in diameter. Stone crabs, caviar, and sushi sat amongst three stations of food. After the cocktail raw bar, guests traveled through the lobby to the ballroom area for the wedding. Heather, however, didn't want the feel of walking through a hotel lobby so they transformed the area into a garden. The path for guests was lined with grass, planted flowers, so many trees that it was an impenetrable forest, fountains, and streams. Guests actually walked through a forest path, through the lobby, to find their seats at the wedding.

Just before the guests entered the ballroom, a huge chandelier loaded with crystals hung overhead. The problem was, Heather didn't like the chandelier. Organizers brought in bushels of baby's breath to fill the chandelier. According to one organizer, one laundry basket sized bundle of baby's breath cost $1.00 at the time, and they used $5,000 worth of baby's breath to fill the chandelier.

For three days, organizers and planners ripped up ficus trees to make a garden rope used as a swag. The two-foot-diameter swag draped the entire ballroom. The beloved mother, Maureen Muss, walked into the ballroom on her way to the rehearsal dinner and wasn't happy with what she saw. She was blunt when she said, take it down, I don't like it. The organizer went upstairs to his room and cried for twenty minutes, came back down, and went back to work. In the end, the old swag filled multiple dumpsters and was replaced with white draping linens. It was beautiful.

The entry of the bride was a breathtaking moment in itself. Heather had once seen a bride enter a church wedding and desired the same effect. When she saw the other bride enter through the church doors, the sun was setting behind her and filled the church with iridescent sun setting pink light. The image was created for Heather with her stepping out of a specially built box outfitted for her with grand entry doors, the inside of which was lit with a specially made lighting show.

The wedding was just one of many parties and celebrations for the Fontainebleau. A party or famous face was often in sight on the grounds even through the Muss years. Gianni Versace was often known to be on site while his house on Ocean Drive was under construction. He stayed under the pseudonym of Paul Beck, his brother-in-law. Donatella used to visit him in the penthouse where he stayed on the 15th floor. He liked the curve of the Chateau and this penthouse relaxed him.

The BG's liked the suite on the 14th floor so much that orchestrators at the hotel had the brothers Gibb sign a large flat piece of glass that was incorporated into the bar top of the suite.

Bleau View opened up with Mediterranean styled foods. The restaurant offered tasteful delicacies as well as a priceless view through the bubble explosion wall of windows that overlooked the rock grotto, pools, and ocean.

The Staircase to Nowhere was put to use in a more updated fashion. The offices for Hilton management were stationed here to make the area useful for more than a parading show of cascading women checking their furs.

Local Laura Lauer remembered her time as a member of the upgraded and revamped health club. "Mr. Muss owned a terrific place. And his wife was just stunning! It was called **The Fontainebleau Spa**, had its own pool and terrific classes. It was priced at under $1,000 per person [in 1988]. In the aerobics class everyone wore leotards and tights. You had a social life at the gym. Everyone sat around with a cup of coffee. It was wonderful, well kept, clean, beautiful. Absolutely wonderful. Under the main floor gym was a sauna, steam rooms, and showers. The pool was inside. Everyone you knew was from there, even now everyone I know is from there."

The 37-story Fontainebleau Tower is used as a visual marker all the way from the mainland.

The tower illuminates the skyline at Indian Creek and Collins Avenue. *Courtesy of Kenneth Glenn, photographer.*

Architectural drawings and construction of the Loews was received with great anticipation by locals. As the first newly built hotel in thirty-one years, the activity was a sign of a positive future.

Stephen Muss built a grandiose new monumental building on the southwest corner of the property. Muss's Fontainebleau Tower was considered the most glamorous and up to date $400 million venture on Miami Beach. At the end of 2004, when Stephen Muss was preparing the tower for completion, he ran a contest. The "Anniversary Contest" was so named as the hotel was approaching its 50th anniversary. Former Fontainebleau guests submitted entries with nostalgic stories reminiscing of the years gone by at the glitzy hotel. Ten winning entries were to be chosen with a free stay as their victorious prize.

Stephen Muss had hit the scene and updated the original property. During that time it was popular to focus on history and Muss made the best of his property. Many of the changes made to the original buildings were reverted back to a more historical status. The escalator that was added to the lobby to siphon people through the hotel and out to the new pool area was removed. Elaborate furniture reappeared. The deep blue carpet that covered the lobby was removed and the signature marble flooring that spoke volumes for architect Morris Lapidus was again revealed. The bow tie was the trademark look for Morris Lapidus.

As far as hoteliers go, Stephen Muss is the original in formidable men. He has a business demeanor that is bold, strong, and capable. Muss ran the hotel successfully for twenty years. Hotelier Stuart Blumberg worked for Muss for five years and described his business sense in detail. "There are no more Stephen Muss'. Stephen Muss saved Miami Beach. He saved the industry. If he hadn't taken the Fontainebleau out of bankruptcy you wouldn't see anything here. He's the original 800 pound gorilla."

As the man responsible for Fontainebleau's resuscitation, Muss created a new era. Muss knew the hotel market was changing and demanded a technological advancement to keep up with the competition. For this reason he joined forces with the famous Hilton family and had them market the hotel. The addition of adding a chain flag to the hotel was an immediate boost. Times demanded a reservation system to book a hotel. Muss wanted to make the Fontainebleau a new hotel with a new image. One of the first things he did after purchasing the hotel was something that makes many people shake their heads.

He put a sign out front.

This sounds basic and simple but the truth was, until that point in the late '70s, no sign reading Fontainebleau existed on the property. The architectural curve of the building was so famous that no sign was ever needed. You knew the building when you got there just by the look.

When you ask a local, you'll find that Steven Muss put money back into the hotel. He changed the rooms, updated, the fixtures, added entertainment, and even upgraded the food to meet the dietary desires of the healthy '80s. People were becoming athletic by the class full. Jane Fonda was releasing her new aerobics tape, a new form of exercise that quickly gained popularity. Leotards and sweatbands became cool to wear even on a trip to the grocery store. Fitness was booming, so Muss responded by putting up a new spa.

The late 1970s were a whole different time for hotels than 1954. In the beginning of the Fontainebleau's life, there was no competition, this was the best and there was no one else. At the time the hotel was brought out of bankruptcy, there was competition worldwide. This was clearly not the only hotel in town.

Stephen Muss was a developer who built, replaced, fixed, and enhanced. Muss was a hard businessman who knew what made money, made a plan, and worked the plan diligently. He wasn't soft and he wasn't easy. He was a man getting a job done. Blumberg described Muss as a man who "taught me how to bust everybody's head across the trees. Every morning Muss walked the boardwalk. He'd start at the spa at 7:30 in the morning, walk to 21st Street, turned around and came back." (Oral Interview, 10/10/07) This was where Muss would get some serious business covered. If he called you to walk with him, you were stuck with him the whole way. Muss could get out his thoughts and you had no exit. "By the time you got back you were mentally exhausted. That's Steve's nature. He could intimidate you, ridicule you, curse at you. You'd get to the office at 9:00 and you were dead for the day. You couldn't function. I learned from him." (Oral Interview, 10/10/07)

Local historian, author, community advocate, and professor Howard Kleinberg refers to Stephen Muss as Darth Vader. This description is a clear example of how the hard-driving businessman, Steven Muss, ran his affairs.

Muss is not just a hard core worker, he's a giver on his own terms. Muss is a philanthropist and has served as chairman of South Beach Temple Emanuel. He began developing properties in 1946 with Alexander Muss, his father, together forming Alexander Muss & Sons. Stephen came to MB in '68 and began developing Key Biscayne, Miami, and the area of Miami Beach.

Stephen Muss was a developer who had changed the coastline of Miami Beach, specifically in the area north of the Fontainebleau. He developed The Sea Coast and Alexander hotels before he moved to the Fontainebleau.

Hotels were becoming more automated at that time. Hotel chains developed a working system that was flowing freely in the marketplace. Stuart Blumberg, President and CEO of the Greater Miami and The Beaches Hotel Association, compared today's hotel marketplace with the time of 1967 when he opened the Hilton (now Castle Beach) in the 5400 block of Collins Avenue. This is the same hotel known as the Playboy Bunny Hotel were Bunnies roamed the property freely dressed in official bunny uniforms, tail and all.

With that job, Blumberg became the youngest General Manager in the country. Blumberg had been with Fontainebleau for years and was serving as Chairman of the Miami Beach Chamber when the city asked him to chair the committee. The committee increased the bed tax collected by each hotel room. The reason to increase the bed tax was simple, the city wanted money for a new hotel. Banks were still not lending money to the South Beach area but the city had a stretch of five acres right on the ocean. A new hotel would allow more rooms enabling larger conventions. The city asked Blumberg to chair the committee in 1991 and 1992.

The City of Miami Beach wanted to loan money to a hotel with the winning bid. After ten years the hotel owner would pay the city off or bring them on board as a partner.

Stephen Muss bucked the deal. He and Stuart Blumberg went head to head on this topic. The concept of another hotel was an emotionally antagonizing venture for Stephen Muss. Until then, the Fontainebleau was a prime property in town. According to Blumberg, Muss said, "You'll never get it done. You're not going to build a bigger hotel in town. I'm the guy. I'm the Fontainebleau."

Bob Tisch knew Stuart Blumberg all the way back from when Blumberg carried his bag at the Eden Roc the first summer it was open. Tisch took a liking to the young boy and told him then he had a future in hotels. As it stands today, Stuart Blumberg is proud that he is the oldest active hotelier in the state. Tisch consulted with Blumberg on the concept. They met for two and a half hours at The News Café discussing the topic. Tisch was on the fence. He wanted to buy the Eden Roc and fix it up, his people wanted him to do the bid with the city enabling them many more rooms. Stuart Blumberg told Tisch, "South Beach is becoming a very hot destination. To have a hotel in the hottest area, it'll be like having an ATM machine with rooms."

Bob Tisch was not 100% sold on the concept but his people and his son John were sold. They put in a bid. Blumberg said, "I look at it full circle. I carried my first bag for the father in '58 and in '98 I helped the father and the son to build the Loews."

Using the same architect that designed the new Fontainebleau Tower, The Loews broke ground in December of 1998 after thirty-one solid years of no new hotels on the beach. Blumberg was right; the hotel is indeed like an ATM with rooms.

At the end of the ten year lease from the city's contract Loews was due to make their decision, pay off the money or partner up with the city. Exactly ten years to the day, Jonathan Tisch walked in and put a check on the city's desk. The loan was paid in full.

Stuart Blumberg and Stephen Muss not only butted heads on the new hotel bidding project; their relationship was severed. Blumberg was under contract and still worked for Muss but the tension was so bad that the two men stayed on opposite ends of the hotel.

Still to this day, Blumberg gives credit where credit is due. He says, "The Fontainebleau always reflects Miami Beach. It's the hotel that complements the Convention Center because it houses so many people under one roof. The Fontainebleau is enormously important. We can't exist on leisure business all year round. Orlando doesn't. Vegas doesn't. Why should we?"

Steve Muss took the broken, crying, partially disrobed queen Fontainebleau and took her back to princess stage. He refurbished, upgraded, and loved her. He wanted to give the hotel a new image. With this he put up a mural that advertised the property. In essence the wall was a six story tall billboard painted in 1986. Muss hired **Richard Haas, a famous trompe l'oeil muralist**, to solve the issue of beautifying the connector wall to the spa.

Richard Haas was born in 1936 in Wisconsin and has perfected his artwork in an eye popping, jaw dropping format. He has the skills for taking a bland wall and making it a breathtaking masterpiece. Haas uses paints to develop a three dimensional quality that leaves you speechless. Haas is arguably the best artist of his time and has used his talent to add beauty on bland buildings throughout the nation. He has transformed buildings eighteen stories tall as well as traditional sized canvases. Each piece is a monumental masterpiece of beauty and style, establishing an architectural fantasy where there once lived bland concrete. In Haas' words he loves to, "take the scarred areas and build them up."

Richard Haas remembers the Fontainebleau project with mixed emotions. "It is bitter sweet to remember the Fontainebleau piece because of its demise. It was for nearly two decades one of my triumphs and I hope-think much of Miami and Miami Beach felt the same way."

When Haas was asked to come do the mural, it was Stephen Muss' idea to add the waterfall to the mural as he just put in this pool system. Haas said,

"The work started out really as a challenge from an architect who was advising Stephen Muss on improving the hotel in 1984." When the men met to discuss the project they had their conference in one of the Fontainebleau's lounges. This wasn't any old lounge in any old hotel. This was one of *those* lounges where the women worked the crowd with their long legs and heaving bosoms in black skimpy costumes. Haas said the meeting, "took place in a Bunny like lounge with the Bunny's in rehearsal while we talked. It was a bit distracting." One thing is certain, Stephen Muss knew how to properly use his grounds for a breakfast meeting.

When Haas reviewed the wall he was held back as, "It had about sixty small windows that opened into the hallways. I said that the site was great but the windows made my doing anything on this area impossible. The architect and Mr. Muss said that would not be a problem, they would simply block up all the windows and better light the hallways behind them. With this in mind I went to work on the design with sketches and models. It was a no-brainer that the thematic feel had to be Art Deco and I was very familiar with Miami Deco at that time. I also immediately thought of a grand opening as there was that great blocked vista looking north on Collins Avenue. I also felt I needed something more and after viewing the great standing Cartydids of Eliel Saarinin's Railway Station in Helsinki Finland which guard that entrance and hold large lit globes, I said that's it. I simply had to transfer them into Art Deco Drag."

The signature shapes that make up the Fontainebleau are still a trademark image, even with the sign out front.

Haas' concept with the chosen mural was one of aesthetic pleasure. The wall that existed was the backside of the end building, the spa. The building at the time was not one solid structure standing as an old historic gem known as The Sorrento. Instead it was a stubby, T-shaped building that stretched much farther than the rectangular shape we see today. The stubby stick of the T was the building that stretched down Collins and butted up next to the Sovereign Hotel. The right arm of the T stretched to the oceanfront and housed the spa. The spa was put in immediately after Stephen Muss' failed Gaslight Club. Lisa Cole said, "The club looked like a whore house, red velvet, dark benches, like an old Chicago steak house. That didn't work so we put the spa in there. It became the local gym." To change the image of the building the hotel tried multiple concepts, including changing the name to The Beach Club and The Yacht Club. Guests didn't like to be separated from the main festivities at the hotel, so they tried to pull the far away building to the forefront of attention. This act was a major project.

The left arm of the T stretched up the curve of Collins. The wall was the back of an internal hallway with hotel rooms stretching the length of the building opposite the hall. The building was old, musty, and smelly. This was before the new thirty-seven-story tower on the corner was built. The Fontainebleau, at that time, consisted of three buildings, the original curved Chateau, the Versailles building which possessed The Spite Wall, and the spa building. Together the three buildings had 1,226 rooms.

The idea for the mural came from the inability to see water from a handful of rooms in the main buildings. For those rooms they looked at a rooftop of the ballroom, fourth floor. The thought of putting a mural on the rooftop, painted to look like ocean water, would give the hotel the ability to use the phrase *water views from every room*. That concept morphed into the mural on the backside of the ugly wall at the foot of Collins.

Muss used his skills with the city, changed the curve of Collins Avenue by swapping land, and put up the mural. Stephen Muss liked to do unusual things and this was no exception. He did it to pull positive attention to the building.

Muralist Richard Haas was inspired with the theme right from that very first visual of the wall to be covered. After the initial meeting with the practicing dancing Bunnies, he and his wife Katherine left the city of Miami Beach only to wait a full year for a response that officially hired him for the project. Stephen Muss called Richard Haas for the project when he found out Haas was presenting a proposal to do another project in South Miami for one of Martin Margulies' malls. Muss wanted the Fontainebleau's mural completed first, so he promptly call Richard Hass to start the project.

The winter season of 1985-1986 was filled with the Fontainebleau for Richard Haas. His wife Katherine and his young infant son spent their days at the pool while Daddy worked.

The **six-story-tall mural was accented with a 110-foot-tower** on the left end. Haas worked diligently and efficiently on the project, completing his masterpiece right before the driving public. This was one of five murals Haas completed for the year. The others were the Autobahn 3,000 Volvo in Fort Worth, Texas, the Coca-Cola World Headquarters in Atlanta, Georgia, 31 Milk Street in Boston, Massachusetts, and the Smithsonian Institute in Washington, D.C.

A PBS documentary *"The City is my Canvas"* covers Haas and his work. The film shows a comedy of bloopers as the wall was dedicated. Haas said, "Several people tried to break a champagne bottle in front of the mural and finally Mr. Muss himself smashed it onto the wall dousing himself and everyone else on the podium in champagne."

The bottle of Cristal Champagne ordered from Food and Beverage for the occasion was a regular bottle of champagne. The organizer didn't know there were specially designed bottles for the purpose of christening a boat or wall. This regular bottle was much too thick to break easily on impact. The moment was tense but has created many humorous tales later in life.

The resulting image of the mural by Haas was breathtaking and mesmerizing. When you drove down Collins Avenue, the wall mesmerized you, holding your attention until the road took the ninety-degree turn to meet up with Indian Creek Drive. This mural was captivating to the point where pedestrians were injured crossing the sidewalk or road while drivers were looking at the mural.

The trompe l'oeil mural created quite a local stir. When they put up the mural, the locals seethed with despising disgust. A wall! An ugly concrete wall! A wall with a mural of the Fontainebleau, gardens, and ocean *that I would be looking at* **if** I weren't looking at this picture of the Fontainebleau, gardens, and ocean. People complained, they nagged, and they threw up their hands in revulsion.

The windows were filled in to prepare the wall for the mural. *Courtesy of Richard Haas.*

World famous muralist Richard Haas created a breathtaking landmark for Miami Beach. *Courtesy of Richard Haas.*

Years later Muss decided to take down the wall to build the thirty-seven-story tower. Funny enough, people were so disgusted with the removal of the wall **that they picketed**.

They yelled and hollered, "Leave the wall! This is Miami Beach! Preservation!"

Stephen Muss wanted to open up the area and make breathing room for the new building. His thought process was easy, my building, my wall, my decision.

Muss made a conscious effort to preserve the **Sorrento**, the neighboring Art Deco hotel immediately south of the Fontainebleau trompe l'oeil. This is the same hotel that was owned by Ben Novack, and is one of the three factors credited with the bankruptcy of Novack.

Stephen Muss wanted to incorporate the Sorrento into the functionality of the Fontainebleau. He preserved the façade of the small hotel with extreme effort, as this project was long after he learned of the historical importance of Morris Lapidus' Fontainebleau. History lives in the La Ronde Room in the Sorrento where countless headlining celebrities like **Tony Bennett** entertained the public in the '50s. The shows didn't end there; in the later years, Julio Iglesias, Gloria Estephan, and Jose Feliciano all performed there before 2001. The famous film *The Bodyguard*, starring Whitney Houston and Kevin Costner, was filmed at The La Ronde Room. In addition, Madonna, Sylvester Stallone, John Travolta, and Rosie O'Donnell have all celebrated occasions in the La Ronde.

The tower has connecting accents to the chateau tower like Morris Lapidus' signature bow tie set in the elevator floors.

Both top floor penthouses have architectural fantasies.

The stone face waterfalls flank the parking pavilion.

Color accents pull in the neon Art Deco qualities.

The front entrance rock grotto waterfalls balanced out Stephen Muss' pool paradise.

The sound from the waterfalls added tranquility to the grounds.

Chapter 18
Fontainebleau Miami

After twenty years of pouring his heart into the Fontainebleau and giving her a new image, Stephen Muss had enough and he tuned his sights on a transfer of hands. Stephen Muss stepped away from his reigning throne at the Fontainebleau and **Turnberry Associates** bought the landmark for $165 million. Jeffrey Soffer, CEO of Turnberry Associates, heads up the new company, Fontainebleau Resorts. Shortly thereafter, the full plans were laid for Fontainebleau Miami. She was boasted in full glory by the company as, "the most dynamic and coveted resort destination on the Eastern Seaboard."

The desires of each and every previous Fontainebleau owner were achieved by Soffer as he defied the Miami Beach government and indeed put gaming into the Fontainebleau name.

He did this by opening a second Fontainebleau in Las Vegas. **Fontainebleau Miami and Fontainebleau Las Vegas** are both independent wonders that capture the spirit of thrill and mix it with dynamite. The properties are different in their own right but carry the same explosive impact.

As Fontainebleau Miami was continuing her development, she was turning into a phenomenon. The thirty-seven-story Fontainebleau Tower II was amplified with grace by the newest addition of an old hotel form.

While under consideration for a makeover, the Sorrento Hotel turned out to be a structurally unsound building. **Architect John Nicholas** was hired for the project after he did such a smashing job with the thirty-seven-story Fontainebleau Suites Tower and the Loews Hotel just south of Lincoln Road. John Nicholas is President of Nichols Brosch Sandoval & Associates and a well-known specialist on the condo-hotel movement currently sweeping the country. Nicholas was also hired by **Eden Roc owners Diego and Inigo Ardid** of Key International.

The Ardids also own the South Beach Marriott and are gifted hoteliers. Nicholas, a favored architect in town, drew up the plans for the Sorrento and presented them to the City of Miami Beach Design Review Board. His efforts were received with overwhelming approval. The old Sorrento was torn down and rebuilt twelve feet to the north of where she originally stood.

Nicholas' plans for the north building were not taken as favorably. He hoped to tear down the building, putting the Spite Wall to bed forever, and start fresh. This was a drastic move to accept for the Historical Preservation Board. In the end, the changes to the exterior structure were minimal.

Turnberry took the Fontainebleau and made it even better. One of the first things they did was close the two original buildings, The Chateau and The Versailles, and sold off all the interior items. A public auction was held where many patrons waited in the four-hour-long-line. Everything was sold from plants, to faucets, to sinks. The end result is a Fontainebleau made up of four buildings, two of which are all suites. The company said it appropriately with their description of "The suitest way to stay," and "The suitest way to play." The original building, **Fontainebleau Chateau Tower** remained intact structurally throughout the extensive construction. The second building stands as a graceful, yet dominating landmark that provides dynamic views of the Atlantic Ocean as well as the twenty-two oceanfront acres of Fontainebleau grounds. **The Fontainebleau Suites Tower** also covers the southwestern-most corner of the property, stands thirty-seven-stories tall and looks like a tall monument with topper pillars. **The Ocean Club** building was the second tower to be built on the southern edge of the property. Ocean Club sits right on the ocean. Together the four buildings make up Fontainebleau Miami.

The third renovation put Fontainebleau on the fast track to fame for the third time in history.

The Fontainebleau Suites Tower was completed in 2005 after ten years of planning and a cost of $400 million. The tower consists of four different unit types, all of which are obviously suites. The Tower Junior Suite, the Tower One-Bedroom Suite, the Tower Two-Bedroom Suite, and the Penthouse Suites are all masterpieces in their own time. Standard luxury is consistent throughout each unit where consistent opulence is comprised of 32-inch flat panel televisions, marble bathrooms, granite countertops, glass showers, and toiletries that induce bath times others will covet. The tower is made up of 462 suites, 230 Junior Suites, 230 One-Bedroom Suites, and two Penthouse Suites. Of the 462 suites, roughly 408 are in the hotel program, which means the owners can use the Fontainebleau to rent out their owned unit as a hotel suite and the owner collects investment income on their unit while they are away from home. All repairs or challenges are taken care of by the Fontainebleau.

The **Tower Junior Suite** is equipped with a king size bed, a queen sofa sleeper, lounging area, and balcony consisting of roughly 500 square feet.

The **Tower One-Bedroom Suite** also has a king size bed, a queen sofa sleeper in a separate living room. A dining area and full kitchen complete a just-like-home feeling with a full-sized refrigerator, stove, countertop and sink area, dishwasher, plus a washer and dryer. This suite hovers right around 1,000 square feet.

The **Tower Two-Bedroom Suite** was a combination of a One-Bedroom and a Junior Suite connected by a hallway giving the apartment the luxurious feeling of a well-appointed house. The unit is roughly 1,500 square feet with two king size beds, two queen sleeper sofa beds, a living room and dining area as well as a full kitchen, three bathrooms, two Jacuzzi tubs, and two glass showers.

A nighttime swim allows a glorious sunset view.

Modern lines accent historical landmarks.

The welcoming entrance both welcomes and eases heavy traffic flow from Collins Avenue.

Morris Lapidus firmly believed a sweeping entry made hotel access inviting.

The new construction phase for six pools engulfed the grounds.

The connecting serpentine awakes the childish desire to explore.

The tower's lower lobby was used as a restaurant through the latest 2007 construction phase.

Shapes, curves, and lines dance together.

Art Deco, MiMo, and Modern designs all flow together appropriately.

The top of the Tower is split into two units, the **Penthouse Suites**. The south penthouse was sold to a private owner in 2007 for $6.4 million during one of the biggest housing recessions the country has ever seen. The hotel program uses the north-facing penthouse.

Each penthouse is a mirror image of the other, split right down the center of the building. One faces south, the other faces north. Both cover the entire length of the building. Space is abundant and the air is clear in this 37th floor masterpiece location. Few places on Miami Beach take you so high in the sky that your ears pop riding up the elevator – this in one of them. For this reason, as well as countless others, the Fontainebleau Suites Penthouse stands in a class of its own.

Currently, the north penthouse is open to a chosen clientele. The luxury tower penthouse incorporates a panoramic view of the glamorous Atlantic Ocean, Indian Creek, Biscayne Bay, the port of Miami, and the city of Miami. Overlooking the vast balcony area, the high elevation and angle of the tower allows perfect viewing into the ocean's near-shore mysteries, exposing manatees swimming in Indian Creek; in the summer months they swim close to the shoreline in the Atlantic. Other ocean wildlife like rays, tarpon, and barracuda are visible to the naked eye. At dawn and dusk when ocean life is most active and feeding, the show is mesmerizing.

A full service kitchen delivers an in home dining dream.

The top floor is dedicated to one north facing penthouse and one south facing penthouse. Each penthouse runs the width of the building. *Courtesy of Fontainebleau.*

The penthouse main living area is dedicated to three full independent zones.

Each penthouse bedroom is equipped with any guest's desire. *Courtesy of Kenneth Glenn, photographer.*

The formal dining zone seats eight comfortably.

The current rates for the 2007 year range from $2,500 to $10,000 a night depending on the time of year. The 4,300 square-foot internal living space is accented with a 3,000 square-foot outside terrace and balcony area. The three bedroom, five and a half bathroom Fontainebleau Penthouse is filled with luxurious Bvlgari amenities, the 1884 Italian company famous for jewelry and lavish items.

The Fontainebleau Penthouse is not only accommodating, spacious, and tranquil, it possesses a unique feature known only to a select few. This locale is home to the most coveted and private of sensual zones on the beach. At the eastern-most edge of the penthouse balcony is a secret worth telling. Hidden behind a raised planter box of foliage is a staircase that takes you one step closer to heaven. This staircase leads to one place only – the exclusive and most discretely private rooftop heated Jacuzzi that rests alongside the glass railing overlooking the ocean.

In this open air, living sea of peace, beside the relaxing rooftop Jacuzzi is a freestanding shower, with multiple showerheads. The stainless steel open air bathing area stands at attention and is ever ready.

Inside the penthouse unit subtle luxuries are standard, like recessed lighting with dimmer switches, crown molding, cordless phones, and wireless Internet. The pristine marble floors are polished to a high gloss shine reflecting the light cascading in through the floor to ceiling, wall to wall windows. Unobstructed views of the ocean, Indian Creek, Biscayne Bay, and city are breathtaking and awe inspiring. Fifteen-foot ceilings raise your level of open-air consciousness.

A separate, private entrance off the kitchen enables the chef to deliver desired delicacies. Staff quarters are off the separate entrance hallway, allowing your nanny or personal aid privacy away from the family. A washer and dryer await your beckoning command. Granite countertops stretch across the vast kitchen as well as bathroom surfaces. Six televisions throughout the unit present the highest technology and resolution.

The master bedroom is one of four bedrooms if you use the office pullout. The master has a private balcony, bar, and sitting area.

The master bath has two private necessary rooms and two separate vanities. *Courtesy of Kenneth Glenn, photographer.*

The private master bedroom balcony overlooks the bay and city views.

Indian Creek stretches in front of the balcony with visible manatee.

Nighttime on the penthouse balcony is a peaceful, breezy paradise. *Courtesy of Fontainebleau.*

Daytime penthouse views are unrivaled.

Storms from the penthouse are an enthusiast's dream.

Ample balcony space wraps both penthouses.

The ocean view from the penthouse reveals rocks and swimming wildlife with ease.

The private penthouse Jacuzzi is a moment to remember.

In the family room area lounging is comfortable and relaxing. A 42-inch LCD flat screen television is only topped by the potential at your fingertips. The television, multi disc changer stereo system, Internet access, and video game console are all incorporated into a television technology extravaganza.

The glamorous kitchen is equipped with storage envied by any chef, upgraded stainless steel appliances, a flat top stove, convection oven, dishwasher, double sink, and granite countertop surfaces able to please any critic. The stainless steel refrigerator supplies ample room for food as well as the continually ready icemaker.

The eating area can be perpetually changing as you have your choice of plentiful balcony space, kitchen bar stools, cozy table for four, and the glamorous dining area where eight people can comfortably dine.

A wet bar and buffet station are ready and able for small personal needs as well as grandiose parties. In addition to the nanny's bedroom off the kitchen, three bedrooms supply peace and quiet to guests. Space is abundant as two of the bedrooms contain 1,000 square feet with the master bedroom encompassing 1,200 square feet. In the master, another 42-inch LCD flat screen television is waiting. This one however is hidden at the foot of the bed and is retractable by remote. Attached to the master bedroom is a private wet bar and a separate private sitting area. The exclusive balcony off the sitting area boasts city views that extend for miles. Separate closets await any new catch from Lincoln Road, as well as any clothes you may or may not need in this all-consuming, ever private, and relaxing penthouse home.

The master bathroom is affixed with two private lavatory rooms; one is completed with a bidet as well as the necessity bowl. A floating raised Jacuzzi bathtub separates a double vanity. A private shower spacious enough for two completes the cherry and marble accented bath.

Back down the hallway, just off the two side bedrooms, an office is ready for the traveling workaholic. This workspace is operational and outfitted with a computer, printer, and fax.

Although the penthouse is able to sleep nine people, it's prepared for comfortably entertaining a party of fifty. The balcony area as well as the penthouse suite itself has ample space for multiple occasions. If ever there was a place to view 4th of July fireworks, this would be it.

With the construction at the Fontainebleau, the numbers of guests have been lower because the two main buildings have been closed. The only usable rooms have been in the thirty-seven-story tower. Even so, the Director of Marketing at the Fontainebleau says, "We sell out the tower on weekends with no three meal restaurant and only the little pool. With 1,000 or more leisure rooms we feel that's pretty strong while under construction."

As the hotel business goes, one weekend fully booked is an accomplishment while cement mixers and flat beds work alongside diggers and bulldozers. Continual bookings are saying something. During construction, food was served in the downstairs lobby area.

Stuart Blumberg, President and CEO of the Greater Miami and The Beaches Hotel Association said, "The Fontainebleau impact coming back [in 2008] is going to be tremendous for the community. The Fontainebleau's importance is because it's the Fontainebleau. Fontainebleau is the flagship hotel of this city. The queen of the city. The Fontainebleau and Miami Beach go hand in hand. One can't make it without the other."

As the business flows, the business flows, just like industry makes more industry. This is proven every month as, "If the Fontainebleau is busy so is Miami Beach," Blumberg said. (Oral Interview, 10/10/07)

The newest tower stands in front of The Fontainebleau Suites Tower and sits directly on the ocean, giving it the appropriate name, **The Ocean Club**, with the incorporated **Sorrento**. This eighteen-story tower was completed in early 2008 and consists of Junior Suite rooms (568 to 817 square feet) and One-Bedroom Suites (813 to 1232 square feet). This tower is also part of the condo hotel program with 286 units making up the tower, 230 of which participate in the hotel program. The tower was completely sold out nearly a year before completion while the rest of the surrounding area was experiencing a real estate freeze.

Standard luxury is made up of granite countertops, 37-inch flat panel televisions, marble bathrooms, oversized Jacuzzi tubs, plush neck hugging bathrobes, and comfy slippers. Housekeeping visits twice daily and nighttime turndown service is available. For Ocean Club, excellence is customary and comfort comes standard. The staff prides themselves in quality service.

Everything in the two original buildings was stripped out, right down to the bare walls. All the walls were removed and the only thing that was left was the concrete core foundation. Morris Lapidus' iconic aspects were preserved with the highest care and delicacy.

The Sorrento was moved 12 feet to the north.

The last building to join the Fontainebleau team, the Sorrento adds historic Art Deco charm.

An arbor provides shade with air circulation. The addition of artistic sun patterns are a bonus to the shaded vantage point.

Today guests can saunter down the same Staircase to Nowhere that Dean Martin descended. **The Miami Beach Preservation Board** was in both pockets of the hotel management staff as well as their bird's-eye view positioned high atop their backs. The concern was that the hotel remains the grand architectural masterpiece put together by Ben Novack and Morris Lapidus. The front entrance is very much the same as it was the day the hotel opened in 1954. The lobby and front entrance are the most preservation sensitive zones in the whole hotel. The original bowtie marble flooring, marble columns, and the Staircase to Nowhere all remain in pristine condition. The guest rooms and meeting spaces have all been altered to meet the needs of today's travelers.

As all the walls were broken out, the room count dropped slightly, not in the manner to change the footprint of the rooms but rather to accommodate today's guests. For example, more families vacation today complete with multiple children and sometimes extended family. This creates a need for more towels, which generates a need for more storage space. The floor plans did not change to alter the rooms, they changed slightly to accommodate the guests.

With all the construction that has taken place at the Fontainebleau, one of the most admirable aspects is the rooms themselves. This cornucopia of options allows for any choice of any type room. Different room sizes range from 250 square feet to 1,500 square feet for traditional hotel accommodations.

All the plumbing and electrical was updated and upgraded to withstand today's technology. The two original buildings were gutted down to their cores structures. Historically prominent features were encased in protective plywood during construction. The new two-story spa with 40,000 square feet of relaxation and peace was built. Even Coconut Willies was upgraded. Current restrictions inhibit building as close to the ocean as the former Coconut Willies building. By law and code, the core cinderblock and concrete frame structure was left as the base foundation for the new ocean front eatery. A two-story restaurant and bar combination that meets the needs and desires of today's travelers will better suit hotel guests in its place.

The Fontainebleau has come through the last dynamic renovation with high praise and even higher anticipation. *Courtesy of Fontainebleau.*

Cabanas consisting of thirty-three units, grass lounging areas, cement lounging areas, Jacuzzis, pools, drinks, music, and anything else your dreams can imagine are as always standard issue at the Fontainebleau. Anyone staying in any of the four buildings can meander from one area to the other with access to amenities.

Even during construction the hotel was booking meetings and conventions. While bulldozers and dumpsters were neatly carrying out their daily duties, the booking and sales staffs were 10% ahead of where they thought they would be. The goal for the management staff was to function at a 50% meetings and 50% leisure status.

While the hotel was under construction, ground floor pools were nonexistent and restaurant facilities became a grand, swanky affair set up in the lobby and common areas. On weekends, the tower with its 1,000 or more leisure rooms was consistently sold out, even during the low season.

The choice to close down and make a major overhaul is always a risky gamble, especially when people own units they call home on site. For the brainpower behind the Fontainebleau, the gamble has proven successful. Eleven different restaurants, three named chef restaurants, a night club operated by PURE from Caesar's Palace in Las Vegas, and more entertains guests like they are royalty themselves. The PURE vibe will flow through with three different entertainment levels with one whole level open to the bottom and balcony arrangement on the third level. The whole establishment focuses on being seen and owning your spotlight.

Today, the Fontainebleau is termed a "MiMo" structure. MiMo is the short, catchy acronym of the "Miami Modern" style of architecture that began just after World War II, running from 1945 to 1965. MiMo is a more modern version of Art Deco. Geometric shapes are the prime building resource, but they are softer in MiMo than in Art Deco. In the Art Deco era rectangles dominated the scene with thrusting finials and decorative toppers pulling your eye to the top of the structure.

In the MiMo era, kidney shaped aspects softly danced with block based concrete flower beds while geometric rectangles stood as the base foundation. On top of these rectangles, the overlaying concrete clothes had morphed, stretched, and pulled at one end creating psychedelic geometric shapes frozen in time as if the building took a drug induced trip. Cast concrete often displayed some sort of simple eye attracting focal point, usually the front entrance.

Coconut Willies was taken to the ground. Current restrictions inhibit building so close to the ocean today. Leaving the base allowed a structure to remain.

Chapter 19
Fontainebleau Las Vegas

As grand as the Miami Beach Fontainebleau is, the concept of the trade name is still flowing strong. Fontainebleau Resorts officially complements Turnberry through the enormous, new Vegas project. A new market is being tapped in the most recent years and that is the market of travel and leisure. A new hotel will fall hand in hand with this concept as the developers open up the new Fontainebleau Las Vegas.

Fontainebleau Las Vegas began moving earth in February of 2007 and is scheduled to open in 2009 at a cost of $2.8 billion. Just shy of 4,000 rooms will make up this new hotel and casino resort that will have a condo-hotel program. The property replaced two formerly well-known locations, the Algiers and El Rancho. The 24.5 acres will be filled with elaborate pools, spas, restaurants, rooms, and a 100,000 square foot casino.

World renowned designers were gathered together to create the most monumental experience to hit the Las Vegas Strip. The luxury casino hotel, situated at the end of the famous strip, is walking distance to the Las Vegas Convention Center, and maintains a collection of the most extravagant aspects and amenities available today. Gaming, entertainment, and luxury live together symbiotically at Fontainebleau Las Vegas. Famed and award winning designers make up a trio of excellence through the three design companies of Bergman, Walls & Associates (BWA), Zapata & Associates, and Steelman Partners.

Bergman, Walls & Associates are Las Vegas experts in design. The team is famous for their design of The Mirage, Paris Las Vegas, Caesars' Palace, PURE nightclub at Caesar's Palace, The Signature at MGM, and Trump International Hotel and Tower. Co-founders Joel D. Bergman and Scott U. Walls have changed the face of architecture. Bergman is the winner of the prestigious Silver Award in 1991 for the Mirage Hotel. *Atlantic City Magazine* voted him as one of their "81 people for 1981" and recently he has been awarded the Sarno Lifetime Achievement Award.

Scott Walls is the lead for the Fontainebleau Las Vegas project. He is a name recognized throughout the world in architectural circles. His work with The Mirage, Treasure Island, and the Golden Nugget has put casino architecture into a market that both entertains and captivates. He has received praise from his work with the American Institute of Architects and the National Council of Architectural Registration Boards. Several team power players add to the mind-blowing project of Fontainebleau Las Vegas, including Leonard Bergman, Robert Fredrickson, and Darrel Wood.

Zapata & Associates is the famed firm that won the National American Institute of Architects Award in 2005. They are masters of their trade in design with their projects of Horizon Tower, Cooper Square Hotel in New York City, Hanoi Marriott National Convention Center, Bitexco Financial Tower in Ho Chi Minh City, Golden Beach House in Golden Beach, Florida, Quito House in Quito, Ecuador, and their award-winning interior at JPBT Advisors in Miami, Florida.

Steelman Partners has brought dynamite to casino design. They are specialists in their field who have helped MGM Mirage and Harrah's Entertainment put their businesses on the map. Their design of the Jade Entertainment Complex received enormous praise specifically from their peers at The American Institute of Architects. They won the People's Choice Awards and the Citation Award for the UN-BUILT Category. The team dominated the 2007 AIA Nevada Excellence in Design Awards Program. The highly experienced company specializes in entertainment architecture.

Fontainebleau Las Vegas is filled with high ceilings and large meeting rooms that cover nearly 394 thousand square feet of functional space. Over 107 thousand square feet is dedicated as pre-function space. A ballroom with 105 thousand square feet is accented with a junior ballroom of 42 thousand square feet, each with ample divisible quadrants. An additional space of over 70 thousand square feet is dedicated to 64 meeting rooms. A full service business center is accented with four permanent boardrooms and flanked by 26 thousand square feet of outdoor function space.

The Las Vegas dynamic addition to Fontaine-bleau Resorts stands 725 feet tall and is made up of 63 floors with 3,889 rooms. A penthouse restaurant crowns the building with 20 thousand square feet of fabulous views and luscious flavors. Most buildings stop with the penthouse but not Fontainebleau Las Vegas. They kept going to add the world's largest rooftop pool.

Fine dining restaurants make up nineteen different choices for dinner destinations. Lounges and bars total twenty different theme experiences while three coffee bars keep the energy level on extreme. The entertainment sector of Fontainebleau Las Vegas is capped off with a 20 thousand square foot nightclub, as well as a 3,200-seat theater. When you need a break you can relax and rejuvenate in the 60 thousand square foot spa or any of the four pools. If shopping is your thing, there's over four acres of desirable stores.

Turnberry has seen enormous success in recent years. From 2000-2005 they have sold over $2 billion in condominium projects in Miami and Las Vegas.

Fontainebleau Vegas has a similar appeal and structure to Fontainebleau Miami Beach in a completely new and revamped property updated to perfection. There will be two major differences creating a completely different atmosphere, the ocean and gambling. Fontainebleau Miami and Fontainebleau Las Vegas generated a press release where Fontainebleau announced the development of the $4 billion project creating both projects. Nine banks have led the project that has changed resort living.

Lisa Cole said it best when she summed up the history of the Fontainebleau by saying, "The owners have been interesting characters but there is something about the land. From the moment that place came to life, it has been unique. The Fontainebleau just brought out the most colorful people. The owners have been very feisty individuals who are not afraid to open their mouths." (Oral Interview, 11/2/07)

The completed Sorento sports an auxiliary entrance.

New interior decor mixes with the MiMo architecture.

The beach scene invites comfort and service.

Warm and inviting seating areas are ample throughout the new spaces.

Beach paradise is perfected, even for the children.

Local children's book authors create sand castle stories with the perfect Fontainebleau sand.

Bibliography

Donated press clipping. Historical Museum of Southern Florida, "Fontainebleau Will Become Private Spa In November," no date or source available.

Donated press clipping. Historical Museum of Southern Florida, Bishop, January 2, 1961.

Donated press clipping. Historical Museum of Southern Florida, *Miami Herald,* November 8, 1961.

http://www.articles.news.aol.com/news/_a/at-80-hugh-hefner

http://www.billmaynes.com/video4.html. Richard Haas interview, 2007.

http://books.google.com/books?id=ErKigdCXUwoC&pg=PA128&1pg=PA128&dg=aretha+franklin+fontainebleau&source=web&ots=6c5RJDK3Mu&sig=H2pXHd9lgTxLjJKsRX_rW_-Alzk#PPA4,M1

http://www.cnn.com/2007/SHOWBIZ/Movies/10/18/obit.bishop/

http://local.aaca.org/junior/mileposts/1924.htm

http://www.southfloridaceo.com.archives/2004_Issues/OCT04/Pages/COVER-MUSS.html

http://www.time.com/time/magazine/article/0,9171,838555,00.html

http://www.travel-watch.com/fontainebleau.html

"Harvey Firestone is Dead in Florida. Rubber Manufacturer Dies in Sleep at His Miami Beach Estate—He was 69." *New York Times,* February 8, 1938.

Biondi, Joann. *A Nostalgic Chronicle of Days Gone By Miami Beach Memories*. Guilford, Connecticut: Insiders' Guide, 2007.

"Ben Novack Sr., 78 Is Dead; Founder of Fontainebleau." *The New York Times,* April 7, 1985.

Buckner, Helen. "Tourism '77: experts say it will be good, 'flat'." *Daily Sun Reporter,* September 14, 1977.

Cohen, Gary. "Swinging at the Fontainebleau." *Ocean Drive Magazine*, January, 2002.

Desilets, Deborah. *Morris Lapidus.* New York, New York: Assouline Publishing, 2004.

Doner, Michele Oka and Mitchell Wolfson, Jr. *Miami Beach: Blueprint of an Eden Lives Seen Through The Prism of Family and Place.* Judenpfad, Germany: Feierabend Unique Books, 2005.

Dozier, Walt. "Fontainebleau sale is delayed 10 days." *Daily Sun Reporter,* November 23, 1977.

_____. "Hotel's fate decided on today." *Daily Sun Reporter,* November 22, 1977.

_____. "Last chance for Novack." *Daily Sun Reporter,* November 26-27, 1977.

_____. "Muss: New man behind Fontainebleau." *Daily Sun Reporter,* December 3-4, 1977.

_____. "Novack tries last-ditch effort to regain hotel." *Daily Sun Reporter,* December 28, 1977.

_____. "Council: Thumbs down to topless beaches." *Daily Sun Reporter,* February 15, 1977.

_____. "Today's sale of Fontainebleau may be delayed." *Daily Sun Reporter,* November 16, 1977.

Fleischman, Joan. "The whole plan is to make south Beach a dream come true." *Daily Sun Reporter*, February 12-13, 1977.

Flynn, Stephen. "Air of Elegance Dims Slowly At Firestone Mansion." *The Miami Herald,* July 25, 1954.

Goldberger, Paul. "Review/Architecture; The Healing Murals of Richard Haas." *The New York Times,* January 10, 1989.

Hanks, III, Douglas. "Checking in, A Look At The History of Miami Beach's Famous Hotels." *The Miami Herald,* December 8, 2005.

"Hotel Strike Spreads." *Sun Reporter*, June 12, 1977.

Kleinberg, Howard. "The Making of Millionaire's Row." *The Miami News,* March 7, 1987.

Kleinberg, Howard. *Woggles and Cheese Holes, The History of Miami Beach's Hotels.* Miami Beach, Florida: The Greater Miami & The Beaches Hotel Association, 2005.

Lacey, Robert. *Little Man Meyer Lansky and the Gangster Life.* Boston, Massachusetts: Little, Brown and Company, 1991.

Lapidus, Morris. *An Architecture of Joy.* Miami, Florida: E. A. Seemann Publishing , Inc., 1979.

_____. *Too Much is Never Enough.* New York, New York: Rizzoli International Publications, Inc., 1996.

Miller, Gene. "Fontainebleau to Close Its Doors to Walk-in Sightseers." *The Miami Herald*, August 20, 1961.

Millstein, Gilbert. "Architect Deluxe of Miami Beach." *New York Times Magazine,* January 6, 1957.

Oral interview, Daniel Hyde, October 15, 2007.

Oral interview, Laura Lauer, September 3, 2007.

Oral interview, Lisa Cole, November 20, 2007.

Oral interview, Michael Aller, October 1, 2007.

Oral interview, Paul Pebley, August 18, 2007.

Oral interview, Pepe Menendez, November 13, 2006.

Oral interview, (email communication) Richard Haas, November 10-11, 2007.

Oral interview, Stephen Muss, August 16, 2007.

Oral interview, Stuart Blumberg, October 10, 2007.

Redford, Polly. *Billion-Dollar Sandbar, A Biography of Miami Beach.* New York: E.P. Dutton & Co., Inc., 1970.

Schneider, Ben. "Story Of New 800-Room Beach Hotel Erroneous." *Miami News,* October 20, 1956.

Schnier, Sanford. "Fontainebleau To Become Spa." *Sunday News,* August 20, 1961.

Stofik, M. Barron. *Saving South Beach.* Gainesville, FL: University Press of Florida, 2005.

Wickwir, Betty. "Masquerade gala 'characters' lively at Deed's benefit." *Daily Sun Reporter,* November 22, 1977.

Woodward, Nancy. "Guests Jam Fontainebleau for Benefit Opening." *The Miami Herald*, December 21, 1954.

_____. "For $50 You Can Get Chicken At Opening of Fontainebleau." *The Miami Herald*, December 19, 1954.